A FIGHTER PILOT
IN BUCHENWALD

Joe Moser's journey from farm boy to fighter pilot
to near starvation in a Nazi concentration camp.

*To Joan
With best wishes
Joe*

Joe F Moser

by **Joseph F. Moser**

as told by **Gerald R. Baron**

All Clear Publishing, LLC
in partnership with

EDENSVEIL

Published By Edens Veil Media

This publication is designed to provide accurate and authoritative information in regard to the subject matter covered. It is sold with the understanding that the author and publisher are not engaged in rendering legal, accounting, or other professional service. If legal advice or other expert assistance is required, the services of a competent professional person should be sought.
> *- From a declaration of principles jointly adopted by a committee of*
> *The American Bar Association and A Committee Of Publishers.*

Please direct any comments, questions, or suggestions regarding this book to:
Edens Veil Media
1319 Cornwall Ave., Suite 200
Bellingham, WA 98225
(360) 671-8708
(360) 647-5351 Fax
www.JoeMoserStory.com

ISBN 978-0-615-22111-3
Printed In The United States Of America
First Edition 0100

I would like to take this opportunity to thank my wife and family for their patience and understanding over the last 63 years. For 40 years they knew little of nothing of what I had been through after being captured. They knew I had served in the military from the picture on the wall. It took many years for me to finally let my guard down and tell them and our friends of my experiences and the horrible events I had witnessed.

In addition I would like to thank Gerald Baron for his patience, wisdom and ability to reach those memories buried so deeply over the years.

I have been asked the same question over and over, "If I was asked to serve my country again, would I do it all over?" My reply — "In a heart beat!" My wife, family, friends and my country mean the world to me.

- Joe Moser

TABLE OF CONTENTS

FOREWORD

For more than 40 years, homeowners in the small communities of Whatcom County, in the far northwest corner of the continental United States, welcomed a quiet, shy, dark-haired man into their homes. He was the furnace guy. For probably hundreds of people in Lynden, Ferndale, Blaine and Bellingham, Joe Moser is still the furnace guy. They had absolutely no idea that the short, smiling and quietly friendly man with the shining dark eyes and big hands was a true American hero. He would greet them with a "How are you?" and mean it. He would offer a thick, meaty hand for them to shake, and when they would ask how he was he would invariably answer, "Real good!" with the emphasis on "real."

For Joe Moser, there were few reminders of his harrowing experiences as a WWII fighter pilot, Buchenwald survivor and POW during the postwar years. One of those few times came in the early 1960s, about 15 years after the war. Joe was working in the shop at Van's Sheet Metal in Lynden, building the pieces for another furnace installation. A voice caught his attention.

"Hi Joe, do you know who I am?"

Joe looked up. The voice struck a chord in him, but when he looked at the man a little older than himself, he did not recognize him.

"Don't recognize me, Joe?" asked the stranger.

"No, I'm afraid not," said Joe, afraid that he would disappoint the man. "I recognize your voice, but I don't know why."

"You should recognize my voice. You sure you don't know me?"

"Sorry," Joe said genuinely. "I don't."

"Does the word 'Link Trainer' mean anything to you? I'm Barry."

Suddenly Joe was brought back to his training days as a fighter pilot. To prepare to fly under the worst weather conditions or to come back to the airfield at night, the pilots had to learn to fly on instruments alone. They trained for this in a tightly enclosed box built like an airplane cockpit with the lid closed and the flight instruments the only thing visible. It was called the Link Trainer, and the voice he recognized was his trainer. It was a disembodied voice that provided instructions, encouragement and corrections. Occasionally the voice would inform them that they had crashed.

Barry had moved to Sumas — one of those small Northwestern towns — and had looked Joe up. But, such reminders of his exciting days as a young, hot shot fighter pilot assigned to fly the nation's fastest fighter plane were few and far between. Joe lived a quiet, unassuming life raising four daughters and a son, enjoying the sports activities of his children with his wife Jean, working and going to St. Joseph Catholic Church in Ferndale, where he had attended since a small child.

None of those customers who watched Joe work quickly and quietly had the slightest idea that in their homes they were entertaining a man who was one of the few on earth who had experienced the darkest parts of Hitler's nightmare. One who had personally experienced the almost unbelievable inhumanity of Buchenwald, who had escaped execution, been treated as a terrorist, and then ended up in the very room from where the most famous escape tunnel in the world had been dug. They could not know of the strength and courage of such a man as he struggled to stay alive during a death march in a below-zero blizzard that lasted days. They could not imagine what a five-day train ride is like in August heat with 90 other frightened men jammed together in a space the size of a small living room — without food or water. They did not know that Joe was a skillful and experienced fighter pilot who did more than his share to achieve victory in Europe. They could not imagine how this gentle, quiet man could have so narrowly escaped the fiery crash of his fighter in a field of French farmers.

In these pages you will hear a story that Joe himself did not share with even his closest family members for decades. And you will know why. I consider myself very fortunate to be the one to share this story with you. I came to this through my good friend, Frank Imhof, who is Joe's cousin, the son of Joe's Uncle Frank. For years Frank told me about Joe, knowing little of his story himself. Finally, in September of 2006, he introduced us, and I quickly agreed to write Joe's story for him.

Meeting Joe and sharing his story has been one of the greatest joys of my life. I hope that I have not only done justice to the events he experienced, but to the quiet strength and beautiful spirit of this seemingly common, ordinary man. It is a continual reminder that none of us are common or ordinary. And yet, from such are born the deeds of sacrifice and courage that make our lives free, prosperous and meaningful.

ACKNOWLEDGEMENTS

My thanks to Joe and Jean Moser for sharing your story and graciously putting up with my delays. To Frank and Patti Imhof for your great friendship and for your support, encouragement and for making this project possible. Finally, to my wife Lynne, our three grown children and seven grandchildren, thank you for your encouragement and willingness to share our too precious time for this project.

In addition to those mentioned above, several others played important roles in getting this book into your hands. Gabriel Rodriguez provided some beautiful portraits of Joe, scanned and prepared most of the images included, designed the initial cover and page layouts; he also helped with the Web site used during the writing. Shawn Olson did the bulk of the proofing, editing and page layout. Brandon Allen did the final cover design, as well as the final page layout and style. Supervising final production was Jason Glover, my longtime colleague at Baron & Company. Our good friend, Patti Ennen, offered her proofing and editorial skills for a final polish. Rob Takamura of Applied Digital Imaging once again was a great help in advising and assisting with the final production and printing.

- *Gerald Baron*

01 FLIGHT LEADER

The day was hazy and hot. August 13, 1944. Even at 4000 feet, it was hot and muggy with a haze that made me uncomfortable. I felt wrapped in a warm blanket when a cool breeze would have been more than welcome. Maybe I was just sweating a little extra that day, which would be understandable since this was one of my first missions as flight leader. There were 12 of us from the 429th Fighter Squadron of the 474th Fighter Group attacking the enemy over France that day. Three flights of four planes each. Our group of four P-38 Lightning fighter planes was given the call sign for the day of "Censor Red." That made me "Censor Red Leader."

I kept cranking my eyes around. Tough to do all jammed up into that cockpit with flight suit, anti-gravity suit, leather helmet, goggles and oxygen mask. I sat on an inflatable dinghy with a parachute strapped onto my back. It was tight quarters with not much freedom of movement. A good set of eyes constantly scanning the skies above, below and all around was the best protection a fighter pilot had. Invariably, it is the enemy you don't see that will get you. So when the adrenalin is flowing, and it certainly was that day, you find a little stretch in all that leather and fabric that otherwise wasn't there.

Sharp eyes were certainly a necessity on bomber escort missions. That day's flight was my 44th combat mission, and many of these flights had been bomber escort missions. In our twin engine fighters we often flew at over 30,000 feet, keeping a close watch on our big brothers below us bringing those explosive loads that we were confident were bringing this horrible war to an end.

Those flights were brutally cold. At 30,000 feet the temperatures are frequently far below zero, and we would cruise at over 300 miles per hour. The P-38s had a bad reputation among many Allied flyers because of the lack of cockpit heat, as well as the problem of the instrument panel and windshield fogging up from condensation, but I loved that plane and still do. In all those dangerous bomber escort missions I never got into a dogfight, in part because our twin-boom plane was a big fighter and very visible to the Germans, who were struggling to keep as many of their fighters alive as possible at this point in the war. They flat out avoided us.

On this particular day, those numbing flights at 30,000 feet were a distant memory and seemed a piece of cake compared to what we had been experiencing over the last few weeks. What once got our hearts pounding like sprinters at the end of a race now seemed like a routine training flight. That's because ever since D-Day — June 6, 1944 — our primary mission had been close air support. It was the primary task of the 9th Air Force, of which I was a part, to attack targets on the ground with machine guns and bombs to support the troops down below who were trying desperately to get more than a toe hold on the European continent.

It sounds kind of simple, and it might seem we had all the advantages. Our job was to seek out and attack almost any enemy target that looked like it might be helping the Germans keep their grip on the west of France. The Allies got on the beach that first day, but then it took weeks to make much progress. The Germans fought hard and brought up all the reinforcements they could. It was our job to disrupt this as much as possible. Anything that moved on the roads or rail lines was a target. The locals were keeping their heads down now as war raged around them, and the trucks, trains, cars, motorcycles were almost certain to be enemy forces.

For the first few weeks after D-Day we flew from our base in Warmwell, England, one of the closest Allied bases to the fighting on Normandy. And while we had the comfort of returning to the safety of England and our Army Air Force accommodations, not all of us were so lucky. In fact, we had lost about one quarter of our squadron by the time this flight on August 13 came along — including our squadron Commanding Officer, Captain Merle Larson, who was shot down on June 21. Captain Larson was a great officer and our most experienced pilot, having flown many combat missions in North Africa. He had been shot down there as well, but had made his way back to Allied lines. We were hoping the same for him now.

It was "flak" that brought the Captain down, as well as most of the others we had lost. Flak — anti-aircraft fire — was feared now more than the enemy flyers. Certainly, there was danger from the German Luftwaffe (Air Force). The Messerschmitt Bf-109s and the Focke-Wolfe FW-190s were occasionally sent up against our bombing and strafing missions. But it was the flak that was the most dangerous and what we feared the most now.

It was flak that was most on my mind as I scanned the ground for targets of opportunity, sweat running in ticklish streams down the side of my head beneath my worn leather helmet. Flak was a concern during our long bomber escort missions, but even the much-vaunted 88 flak gun could reach no higher than 25,000 feet. We could put up with an awful lot of freezing up there at 30,000 feet as we watched the dirty, dangerous gray puffs about 5000 feet below us. How many times on those missions I considered how lucky I was to be safely above those bursts that sometimes were so thick it seemed you might be able to jump from one to the next.

We were about 20 minutes from our base near Isigny-sur-Mer. Our base was called Neuilly because it was close to a small village called Neuilly de Foret. I call it a base, but it was not much more than farmland that had only a few days before been leveled and the beautiful hedgerows bulldozed out to make a landing strip for our fighters. Steel mat had been rolled out for the runway and we were in business. On August 6, just a week before today's flight, we had landed at this new farmland base and were still in the process of settling in. It was great to be on the mainland, and the days were filled with exciting reports of the now rapid Allied advance through France.

Our new base was very near the beaches that had now become known around the world as Utah and Omaha. Isigny is just south of the bay or inlet that divided these two great battlefields. Two months earlier, our fellow soldiers from America, England, Canada and other places had landed on this ground and on Utah beach particularly. A great many of them left their dreams, hopes and blood behind.

It had taken weeks for the Allies to get very far off the beaches. After miserably hard fighting through the farm fields and hedgerows of Normandy, the U.S. First Army under General Hodges and Patton finally broke through the tough defenses and started their big sweep east toward Paris. The breakout occurred right at the end of July, and here we were in the first week of August landing our planes and planting our feet on this newly liberated farmland.

It felt strange and a little unsettling to be seeing France at ground level. Certainly we had seen a lot of it from the air in the days following D-Day, as we bombed and strafed enemy targets. But now we were in France, living in tents on the land that had only recently been some farmer's home and livelihood. I thought about my family's farm back in Ferndale, near the Canadian border in Washington State. How would I have felt to see the land I so loved torn up so that these noisy machines could land? But the few French that we occasionally met after arriving made it very clear that they were most happy to see us, and they were eager to rid their country of the much-hated German occupiers.

The haze was heavy enough that even at 4000 feet, we could not see far ahead of us. I worried a little that it wouldn't take much flying time for us to lose track of each other. Staying tight together was our best protection in these dangerous circumstances — as protection against both the German fighters and the flak. Our flight of four planes was organized into two groups, each with a leader and a wingman. The wingman's job was to follow the leader down fairly tight behind and off to the right. It was a method that had been developed for most effective dogfighting, because while the leader was engaged in attacking an enemy, the wingman would continue to search the skies for additional enemies and would sneak up behind the attacking plane. This formation was also very important during these bombing and strafing runs, in part because if something happened to the leader, the wingman would know what happened, what the problem was, where it happened and could call for any help that was needed and let the ground troops know where a flyer had gone down.

If I spotted a good-looking target, I would call the attack, and our four-plane group would go down together. First my wingman and I, followed closely by the second leader and wingman. But not too closely, as Captain Glass had just lectured us. One of my squadron mates, Lt. Moore, had been killed not long before. He was flying wingman on July 14 and following his leader in for a bombing run on a bridge. The leader let the bomb fly when they were very low, and the concussion from the explosion flipped Moore's big fighter over, causing him to crash immediately into a stone building. A beautiful, powerful flying machine and another brave, young 21-year-old gone forever in a ball of exploding fuel and metal. There were all sorts of ways this kind of fighting could get you.

I was very aware of all the possibilities that morning at the pre-flight briefing. Our routine was pretty simple. In the afternoon, the list would appear on the wall of the briefing tent naming the pilots who were assigned to fly the next morning. A full squadron had 16 planes, but most days it would be good to get 12 in the air due to repairs, pilots needing rest or other reasons. My name was on the list for the bombing and strafing mission on August 13. It was Sunday, but there was no day of rest during this activity we called war.

At 6:30 in the morning, a sergeant would come through the tents waking up those of us who were scheduled to fly. I'm a farm boy, so 6:30 was hardly early for me. We'd pull on our tan GI shirts and green GI wool pants. Over that went our flight suits — basically coveralls. Then we'd pull on our boots. But in this warm weather, we didn't wear our big, heavy GI boots that went well up our calves. Instead we wore our lighter ankle-length leather shoes. I stepped out of the tent and immediately felt that this would be one of those sweltering mid-August days. I scanned the sky and noted the haze.

Unlike at Warmwell, we were served breakfast out in the open, cooked over campfires. Still powdered eggs and some black stuff they tried to get us to think was coffee. Sometimes the enlisted men doing the cooking had a hard time getting the fires going in the morning, so they fueled the flames with some French cognac which definitely got things heated up in a hurry. Food was on my mind almost all the time, and I thought back later on all the complaints we made about the rations we were given. To find out exactly what we were assigned, we headed to the briefing tent at 8:30 a.m. The day was already approaching hot as we sat down for the briefing.

The briefing was done by Major Burl Glass. The major had been our CO — our Commanding Officer — of the 429th since it was created in Glendale, California on August 1, 1943, one year earlier. He was a captain then and made major on a day I will never forget — on the return of our first fighter sweep as a unit over France. That was April 30, 1944. So long ago it seemed now.

The major was a respected pilot and a respected leader, but frankly, we were scared to fly with him. He was a "natural" pilot in the sense that the plane just seemed to become part of him, and that is a tremendous advantage in a lot of flying circumstances. But it was a big disadvantage when flying by instruments in bad weather. The simple reason is that the seat of your pants fools you in these conditions. You could swear you are flying straight and level, then you bust out of the clouds and you find yourself in a climb that leads to a stall or in a steep dive heading for the ground. This is exactly what happened several times when the major was leading a flight. We'd run into bad weather, and the next thing you know the whole flight was cockeyed and coming out of the clouds in a dangerous dive or other uncomfortable and dangerous attitudes.

But the Major wasn't leading this mission today, and the briefing was so routine that we could have almost repeated it from memory. Col. Wasem — CO of the 474th Fighter Group — was leading the mission, but I was to be flight leader of our group of four planes. When the major announced that I was to be flight leader that day, I found myself paying a little more attention than normal. I had been promoted to First Lieutenant in July — an accomplishment which I attributed both to the fact that I had flown a lot of missions and, sadly, because increasingly our squadron was being filled with new, less-experienced pilots to replace those who had been killed or shot down. Sometimes success can be attributed to just surviving — a simple truth that became painfully clear to me in the months ahead.

My wingman was assigned by Major Glass, and I glanced over at him. He looked straight ahead at the briefing map. I didn't know him well as he was one of the replacement pilots, and so I couldn't read his reaction. Did he think, Oh great, this idiot is going to lead me into trouble? He had been in the unit for a couple of months, but I had flown with him on escort missions and he seemed an OK pilot. But for some reason I was a little uneasy. It wasn't unusual for me to not know him well, as I am a pretty quiet guy and tend to keep to myself a fair bit. There were a few pilots I considered good buddies, particularly Ernie Nobly from Minnesota. Ernie and I learned to fly P-38s together, and we had stayed together all through training and into the war.

The mission was what was called "armed reconnaissance" or "armed recces." Our general target area was Rambouillet, a good-sized town just 10 miles southwest of Versailles and only about 25 miles from Paris. The German reinforcements being brought in to try to slow the now rapid Allied advance would be mostly coming from this direction. We would look for armored units, supply trucks or trains, officer's staff cars or just about anything else that looked to be a likely military target.

"If it moves, smash it," said Major Glass. The days of trying to determine first if the vehicles on the road were German or French countrymen were coming to an end. Now we had orders that anything that moved was German.

"Keep your eyes on patches of woods located near roads or rail lines," the major said, as if we needed reminding. "Let's find some more Tigers."

A couple days earlier, on Friday, August 11, we had received word of several German Tiger tanks on a road nine miles east of Domfort. These were the big boys that could do incredible damage to our own tanks and infantry. We were sent up at 1500 hours (3:00 p.m.) on a tank-busting mission, each plane loaded up with two 1000-pound bombs. There were 13 of us on the mission with Captain Pappy Holcomb as the flight leader. Pappy had taken over as Squadron Operations Officer for Captain Larson, who was now Missing In Action. We found the tanks, but they had been spaced out and were trying to hide in some trees. A few minutes later, the little forest where they hid received 26,000 pounds of high explosives, and we flew back satisfied that by taking these big guys out we had saved some American lives.

I looked at the map carefully. Our flight would take us in the direction of Dreux. Several P-38s had met their doom in the Dreux-Chartres area — including Captain Larson's. I wondered what had happened to him, if he made it out OK and if he would be one of the lucky ones helped by the French underground to get back to our unit. This is exactly what happened to Hugh Thacker, who was shot down on May 7 and five weeks later called up from London. He had a harrowing trek through the Pyrenees into Spain, helped all the way by brave French men and women.

By 10 that morning we had taken off. I never really got over the thrill of putting my hand over the twin throttles of the fighter and feeling the vibration and acceleration as the power of almost 3000 horses pulled me over the rough runway and into the air. We headed almost due east on a course that would take us toward our target close to Paris.

Now that picture of the map was in my mind as I searched the French countryside below me. Many hours of briefing and studying the maps made the terrain and the towns below quite familiar. It seemed so quiet and peaceful. The fields were laid out in uneven patches, hardly ever square. They meandered through the countryside, separated by the impassable hedgerows in a way that seemed at once haphazard and still carefully ordered. As we passed over small villages I thought of the French families below. I was always fearful that the two 500-pound bombs that we carried under our drab green wings would drop in their vicinity, and yet I was so hopeful that they would do their worst and drive the Germans back to their own borders and out of the war. Much can be hidden even from trained eyes at 4000 feet, and I scanned intently at every road, at every crossing and at every small patch of woods.

I saw a rail line and scanned up and down the line as far as I could see for any trains. Nothing. I was getting frustrated. I didn't want this day, one of my first as flight leader, to end without finding something worthy of receiving the load we were carrying. In the hot haze a few miles ahead and to my left, I thought I caught sight of some trucks. I banked slightly north, and my wingman and second group followed. We were a few miles northeast of Dreux. A convoy? I still couldn't be sure. It was, and my heart skipped a beat. Trucks. Several of them. They were standing still on a road that led into Houdan. Standing out in the open. Well, that's not smart, I thought. I didn't stop to think that it might be too obvious. That a heavy anti-aircraft battery might be waiting for us.

"Censor Red Leader," I called into the mike, adrenalin running high now. "Truck convoy on the road. I'm going in." At that point all I thought about was my target. As I had done so many times before, I centered the target in my windscreen and kept it there as the fighter picked up speed in the dive. A 40-degree dive would quickly get the craft flying at over 400 miles an hour, and the trucks were coming up quickly. There was no doubt now that it was a German convoy — the day's covering haze was growing lighter as I screamed down. My fingers were on the bomb release, and I hoped to see the satisfying explosion as German equipment, ammunition and fuel erupted.

Instead, what erupted was flak. Puffs of smoke were suddenly coming from guns on both sides of the trucks. "Oh shit," I said, using the only swear words a Catholic farm boy could use. It was a trap, and I had fallen right into it. Now explosions were bursting around me as I hurtled toward my target. I was down to nearly 200 feet, just ready to release my bombs when

I felt a tremendous shudder as a 37 millimeter shell ripped into my left engine. Banking sharply left and beginning the pull out of the dive, I felt my zoot suit do its job, pumping with air and keeping blood flowing to my brain. I glanced at the engine. Fire was already streaming behind. Still the flak bursts continued, and I turned the momentum of the heavy fighter into as rapid a climb to the northwest as I could manage.

I turned to look for my wingman, hoping he had escaped the unexpected barrage. No sign of him. I swiveled my neck left and right hoping not to see a burst of orange on the ground or a smoking fighter. Nothing. I looked for the rest of my flight. No sign of them. I was alone and my plane was on fire. For an unexplainable reason, he had not followed me down to the attack.

"Censor Red leader. My left engine on fire. Returning to base," I called. It sounded routine, though my heart was pumping wildly. I heard no answering call. Where were those guys? I was sure they saw me get hit, would follow me and see that I made it OK if I did have to jump. But the haze was thick. I couldn't see them, and I realized they could probably not see me. Why didn't my wingman follow me?

Now I was all business. Training kicked in, and I knew what I had to do. Shut down the left engine, and hope that the air flow over the still speeding plane would put out the fire. I feathered the propeller, stopping it from free-wheeling to reduce drag. Full throttle on the right engine to get as much altitude as possible and head west.

I saw a road below me. I still had those 500-pound containers of high explosive beneath my wings and a raging fire a few feet above them. I had to drop those bombs, and when I saw the road I knew it was safe to drop them without hurting or killing any French kids in the process. Now, head west, back to the American lines. Do anything to get this bird past enemy territory. The fighter was straining to climb as I pulled back on the half circle wheel and held heavy pressure on the left rudder to keep the ball centered and the plane flying on one engine. I looked at the engine, praying that the fire would die down or go out. It was growing. I kept up the steep climb. I wanted as much altitude as I could get. That way, if I managed to get the fire out or even slowed down, I would have plenty of time to get to the American lines and maybe even the base. 1000 feet, 1500 feet. The altimeter was climbing steadily, but now only 1500 of those horses were working, and the fiery mess on my left was not helping at all, just holding me down.

Still the fire grew. Just a little bit further, I thought. I was shaking, but I knew I could make it back. I started thinking of the plane's belly landing on one of those soft fields, with American soldiers running up to me, pounding me on the back and personally thanking me for helping take out those tanks and ammunition trains. 2000 feet, 2500 hundred. I was always confident, all through training, all through the war. Scared to death, yes, of course, but I was sure I would make it through each flight, each encounter, each flak burst. Even now, with my plane on fire, I was sure I would get home and see my family again. I could feel the heat from the fire getting stronger.

"Oh, come on," I thought and prayed. Just a little further. A few minutes more and I can put this thing into a glide and get back to friendly territory. But the flames were now not only engulfing the engine, they were walking up the wing right toward the cockpit.

Five minutes more. The altimeter showed 3000 feet. But I was starting to burn. How many times we young pilots had thought of burning up in our cockpits. It was a fate we hardly dared allow into our heads, but I knew that hundreds or thousands of brave young men had ended their lives just this way. And now I was burning. It shouldn't be happening to me.

I reached up and pulled the canopy release. The plexiglass canopy blew off and a rush of hot air hit me. Now I thought about bailing out. How much heat can I take, I wondered. Not much more. Bailing out of a P-38 was a very dangerous exercise, and too many pilots had been killed doing it. At high speed, you would fly up and over the broad tail plane that connected the twin booms. But at low speed, you had a very good chance of hitting the tail. More than one crashed P-38 was found with its pilot still caught on the tail. How many more had been knocked out by the impact so that no parachute opened? My speed was low now, having done a maximum climb to over 3000 feet on one engine. There was only one way to get safely out of this plane, and that was to flip it upside down and fall out.

"Remember to unstrap your harness first," the instructors told us. "But not your parachute." I thought about all that now as I pulled the buckles loose from the straps that held me tight to my seat. Falling out without a parachute would be almost as bad as burning up in this plane, and burning up was very much a reality right now. 3200 feet. Five more minutes and I'd be over the lines.

With a loud crack, the glass of the window on the left side exploded and bits of glass flew everywhere, including down my back. A searing piece found its way past my helmet, under my flight suit and burned a small hole in my back, but I never felt it. The scar I still carry is my reminder not only of a focused mind, but of the intense heat I was feeling at that time. With that last message, I knew I had no choice. The wild flames were at my elbow and I had to go. I turned the doomed plane over onto its back and dropped out.

02 COME ON!

Once I turned the plane over and dropped through the plexiglass canopy, I immediately felt the wind suck me back toward the tail of the P-38. That was my single thought now. Watch the tail. I didn't want the Germans or the French farmers below to come across the burning hulk of my fighter with me toasted like an overdone marshmallow, my parachute draped over the tail. And I didn't want to be flung into it by the rushing air, knocked out cold and not able to pull the ripcord on my 'chute. Hitting the ground 3000 feet below without a parachute did not seem a good way to die either. Because my doomed fighter was climbing on one engine, its airspeed was only about 160 knots. At that low speed, the danger from the tail was greatest. Over 240 knots and the wind would likely pull me clear. But not now.

As soon as I felt the wind push me, I craned my neck as far back as I could to watch the tail. When I saw it fall away, I would pull the cord. There it was. That flat blade between the twin fuselage booms of the P-38; the booms, extended narrow cones ending into flat, egg-shaped tail fins with rudders. Yes, there it was. Should be falling away any time now. The sky was the gray-yellow-white hue of a muggy, mid-August day. My neck was craned back as far as I could see. My hand had instinctively moved up to the parachute harness until I felt the ring of the ripcord firmly in the grip of my right hand. I needed to pull it and pull it soon. With the power cut, the fighter with its whole left side now engulfed in wind-fanned flames had slowed even more, but then once it inverted it began to pick up speed as it headed for its final destination– French farm soil. The tail was still there, floating down with me. What was going on? The rapidly increasing pressure from the wind was pushing me back further. I thought of looking down to see where I might land, but I kept my eyes locked on that tail.

"Come on," I said out loud to the tail. It is time you go away. I can't pull this thing until I am clear. Why aren't you leaving? Why are you going down with me?

Faster and faster we dropped. "Come on," now more a command than a question. It was getting urgent. That tail was supposed to leave. Float away. Why was it still there? "Come on!" I shouted at it. The wind was pushing on me, and I felt it would push me right into that flat, metal blade. Still the tail floated with me, and still I craned my neck as far as I could to keep it in sight. Now, for the first time I began to get a sense of panic. The tail was still there. Why? It should leave. It should float away. The pressure from the wind felt it could pull my body apart, torso from leg. Something had to give and had to give soon. "Come on!" I said quietly, this time a desperate prayer. "Come on!" And then, suddenly, release. The tail floated away, and I jerked on the ripcord with a ferocious sense of relief.

The silk billowed out, and for the first time I saw the brown-green earth below me. My God, right below me! I was on top of it. I would hit in seconds! The silk began to open and fill with air, and my body, hurtling toward the ground at over 400 miles an hour, was viciously jerked by the harness to a near stand still. At that instant, I heard a terrific "crump" as my fighter dove into the ground and exploded into a huge ball of dust, fire and black smoke. A split second later I hit the ground. Hard. Still gyrating wildly under the just-opened parachute, my legs hit first and felt they might break under the collision. Then I fell heavily onto my butt and back. Stunned for a moment by the sudden collision with earth, I laid there for a moment trying to decide if I was still alive.

It didn't really hit me until much later what had happened and how close I had come to riding my burning fighter all the way down into that fiery death. The toe of my leather GI boot had caught on the canopy as I dropped through. Instead of dropping into that murky sky, I was firmly fixed by one foot to the stricken plane. My only thought was the tail and clearing it before pulling my parachute, but I had ridden that plane down, upside down as it went into its accelerating death dive. The extreme pressure from the wind, faster than any hurricane, tore the heavy leather and freed me at the last possible second. My single-minded concentration on the tail kept me from certain panic and probably helped save my life. If I had realized my toe was caught I probably would have been watching that instead of watching the tail and pulling my ripcord the instant I was clear. I would have plenty of time in the dreadful days ahead to think about this narrow escape and the sense that any time I had on earth, any time at all, was a miraculous gift from the Giver of Life.

But now there was not time to think. I moaned as I picked myself up from the freshly cut grain field and saw the billowing black smoke from my plane. My sorrow at having lost such a wonderful machine and faithful fellow warrior was immediately overcome by a gut wrenching fear. The plane had exploded practically on top of a French farmhouse. From where I stood, less than a quarter mile away, it looked as if the house was burning with the plane. Oh my God, I thought, as I stared at the sickening sight and slapped the French dust off my flying suit. What if I killed some people in there? What if there were kids in there? I should have stayed with that plane. I should have just crashed landed it somewhere where it couldn't hurt anybody. I was trying so hard to save my own life, to get back to the lines, but I might have killed some poor innocent people just thinking about myself. I kept looking at the house, hoping that I could see someone running out of it safe, unhurt.

Throughout all my experiences, including the horrible days ahead, there were few sights that caused me more nightmares in the many, many years following the war than watching my plane burn next to that little stone house. The image was seared into the deepest part of my brain, and no matter how hard I tried I couldn't remove it. The nightmares of what that crash might have done to a French family, probably a family very similar to my own who had come to America from Switzerland only a generation before, continued for over 40 years. They would not stop. They did not get better. The burning plane and the image of burning kids haunted me night after night, until I finally found relief one memorable day in 1988, which I will explain later.

The column of black smoke in the heavy August air would be a beacon for the Germans. Any minute they would arrive to try and find me. "I can't believe this," I said to myself. It just didn't seem possible. I looked around now and saw that I had landed in a field that had recently been harvested. In that field, farmers had been busy shocking the long stalks of oats. Peaceful-looking shocks dotted the field, including right near where I landed. I dropped the parachute harness from my shoulders, but I still did not feel the burn on my back from the shattered glass. That would come later. My legs were rubbery, stiff and painful, but other than that I knew I was uninjured. I quickly pulled on the parachute lines and gathered the clean, white silk toward me. I needed to hide it and there was no time to waste.

Now several of the farmers had come up to me. They grabbed my hand with big smiles and clapped me on the back. For some, it was perhaps the first chance they had to say thank you to the Americans who were rescuing them and their land from over four years of darkness and fear. But I could also see fear on their faces as they kept an eye on the narrow dirt road that ran at the edge of the field toward the village of Marchefroy. A couple of young teenage boys starting grabbing at the silk, pulling it all together. I quickly pulled off my leather helmet, undid the clasps that held my zoot suit–anti-gravity suit– and then unzipped the long front zipper from my flight suit.

I could understand a little French when they didn't talk too fast, and one farmer, I would find out much later that his name was Francois Vermeulen, seemed to take charge. In the field were 20 or 30 farmers, and when the Germans came, they and I hoped I would blend in with the rest. The plan was simple, I'd become just another French farmer. But I had to get rid of anything that made me stand out or look like a pilot. The shocks were big enough so that one could hide my parachute, flight suit, helmet and all the other paraphernalia of my recent, now past, occupation. I was down to olive green GI pants and tan tee shirt. I kept my boots on, with the missing toe leather on my left boot. All the more realistic I ridiculously thought. Just a poor French farmer.

The young farmer who had taken command told me to stay with him. The small crowd that had gathered around me was to disperse, get back to work. And not a moment too soon. No sooner had I joined the work of gathering up the stalks of cut grain, I heard the distant sound of a motor. Motor car? French? No, I realized. We had just received orders that we were to strafe anything that moved around here. It was only the Germans who had any form of transportation now, especially any form of motorized transportation. It was definitely German. I looked up and over my shoulder. I would keep my back to them at all times, even though my swarthy complexion and black Swiss hair made me look southern European and would help me blend in. I saw the dust cloud moving fast from the direction of the village, not more than two kilometers away. I worked away, my back strained by the hard fall, tightened against the stooping over required to gather up the grain. I was careful to keep pace with my fellow farmers, old and young men and women, children and teenagers, who would steal quick glances at me and smile. Nervous, fearful smiles. But smiles that conveyed so much of what they had endured in the past four years.

Some stopped now to look at the dust cloud as it quickly advanced in our direction. I glanced as well, not wanting my over-industriousness to give me away. It was a motorcycle. I could now hear the distinctive two-cylinder motor sound, and soon after I could see the helmeted rider keeping just ahead of the billowing dust. Sidecar, I could see now. Two helmeted Germans. My heart pounded again, but now, without the activity required in bailing out of a plane, I could feel it and swear I could hear it. Perhaps the farmers could too. Might the Germans sense this kind of fear even from the road? The motorcycle continued at top speed right toward the plane. The flames were gone but dark smoke still rose into the late morning air. It was about 11:00 a.m. How strange, I thought. Breakfast near the beach. Briefing. Into the air at 10:00 a.m. Shocking grain in a French farm field an hour later. Now, looks like lunch with the enemy.

We kept working. Sweat was turning my tan tee shirt dark — sweat from the exertion and more sweat from the fear, which tasted like dust in my mouth. The two German soldiers dismounted near the plane, which was about 300 yards away. I kept working but kept a close eye on them. Run? I looked over at the farmer who had given the orders. He kept his head down and waved at me to keep working. Right. Stay with the group. It was my best chance right now. The Germans walked all around the plane. They looked around the house. They stopped and looked out into the field, right toward our group. What if they came out here? I glanced over again. The farmer kept working, kept his head down and I did the same. What would a bullet feel like? I didn't want one in the back. Yet, facing a barrel seemed unpleasant. I kept picking up the stalks of oats and stacking them into the growing shock.

'Hruuumph!" I heard the motorcycle start up again. Keep working, keep working. Amazingly, the two drove off through the same diminishing cloud they had created with their arrival. Now a new sluggish dust cloud billowed up as they made their way back to the village. I felt myself get weak and at the same time my heart get lighter. Two close calls in one day. Thank you dear Mother.

The noise was gone now, and the cloud slowly dissipated in the noontime air. Several of the farmers gathered around. The farmer who had taken charge gave instructions in French to the others, and I could catch enough to see the plan evolve. There was a patch of woods about a quarter mile away, northwest of where my plane landed, past the road and at the edge of the next field. Two young men in their late teens, maybe just a little younger than me, were to hide me. One was the younger brother of the farmer who was running the show. He pointed at the nearby woods.

"Non," the older farmer said. He pointed beyond that, more due west. There was a larger woods. Two kilometers away. The Germans would send a search party, he was sure. And they would search the nearby woods first. Much better to get to the farther woods. If we could make it.

The farmer looked at me and then at my belt. "No," I said, anticipating his question. "No gun."

Most pilots carried the .45 pistol they were issued, but at this stage many opted not to. Too dangerous. If you were caught with a gun, we were told, they would likely just shoot you. There were too many stories of pilots who were shot down or maimed because they were carrying a gun, so now we were advised not to. I wasn't going to get shot down anyway, I thought, so I left my pistol at home. If I had it now, I would have to do what most pilots who bailed out did and that is bury it.

The decision was made. We'd head for the woods two kilometers away. My years of running nearly five miles every night after football practice from Ferndale High School back to our farm just off the Slater Road and right next to the Lummi Indian Reservation came to mind. This would be easy — even with my banged up legs and back.

We started off at a good trot and crossed the little dirt road that the motorcycle had used just 15 minutes before. I felt a smile come across my face as I ran. Maybe this day wouldn't end so badly after all. I'd get to the woods and then wait until night. Maybe these brave young men would stay with me. It was only 60, maybe 100 kilometers, back to the American lines. Who knows, as fast as they were moving, maybe I'd just hide out in the woods for a couple of days, and I'd find myself in American hands. The Germans would be too busy trying to save their own necks to worry about me. I felt halfway home already just running across that field.

Then, what was that? A motor? No, couldn't be. Not that motorcycle again. Run. Run fast. We looked back. The dust cloud billowed up again from the direction of the town. Run! Now there were just three of us and no hiding as farmers. We were obviously running away for a reason. Guilty and visible. And they spotted us. Still we ran, looking for cover. There was no place to hide. Just open field, and now the motorcycle was bouncing crazily through the field behind us. It came closer. I thought for a moment I might hear the crack of a rifle. Instead, over the roar I heard, "Halt! Halt!"

The boys stopped. Come on, I wanted to say. Dodge. Run like a halfback. But I couldn't leave them. I didn't want a bullet in the back either. I stopped, turned and walked up to the boys.

The boys were staring into the muzzles of two rifles. One of the boys looked at me, and I knew what he was trying to say. Say nothing. Keep quiet. We had been trained to pretend to be deaf and dumb if we were captured. No problem. I was a quiet guy anyway. Avoiding the temptation to talk would be easy.

"Wo bist du?" they asked roughly, one now standing back a pace with his rifle leveled at the young man standing directly in front of me and the other one. The two young men reached into their pockets, which drew a nervous reaction from the soldiers. The boys produced their identification papers while the first soldier looked at me. I looked back dumbly. They exchanged words with the boys and I could tell through the mix of German and French that the brave young Frenchman was telling them that I was deaf and dumb. I'm sure the look on my face was convincing.

The first soldier handed the boys' papers to the second soldier, who studied them. Then the lead German moved the young men aside with his rifle and came to me. With the other rifle pointed at my chest, the first soldier searched my pockets. Nothing. I had hidden everything under the shock of grain. He reached toward me, touched my sweaty tee shirt feeling metal against my breast bone as I breathed heavily from the run — and adrenalin.

Dog tags! He reached roughly under my shirt, and jerked them over my head. He looked at me and laughed.

Then he looked around, behind us, up and down the field.

"Wo ist der andere flieger?" he asked.

I looked at him with a blank stare. It was easy to play deaf and dumb when you didn't know what they were saying. I looked around to see what he was looking for. He looked at me questioningly, and I returned his stare blankly. Flieger was pilot. He was looking for another pilot. Suddenly I noticed these two Germans were not alone. The field was crawling with them. They were emerging with rifles in hand from the small woods we had opted not to try and hide in. Perhaps 100 Germans were now searching up and down the fields.

"Der andere flieger?" he demanded. More words were exchanged with the French boys and I could tell they were not polite requests. The Germans were certain another pilot, or maybe more crew members, were hiding nearby. They must have thought the P-38, admittedly a big plane, held two pilots. Perhaps they only judged it by the size of the crash site and thought it was a bomber. They threatened all of us with execution if we did not tell them where the other flyers were. I just looked at him and shrugged my shoulders. Playing dumb was getting to be a habit.

Several of the Germans now took the boys off into a different direction, while another group motioned me to start moving. I looked over at those two French lads. What would happen to them? I was too preoccupied at the moment with my circumstances, but for 43 years after this moment, I thought of those boys. Thousands and thousands of times. In my dreams, while eating dinner, while working on furnaces. Tens of thousands of prayers for their safety. As for me, I was now a POW, marching toward Marchefroy, securely in the hands of the enemy I had been trying to destroy just an hour before.

03 MARCHEFROY

Marchefroy has such a sweet and peaceful name. It is the same today as it was before the Germans invaded in 1940. Just a handful of homes and outbuildings. A few small shops. One narrow street separating the picturesque and ancient stone houses and buildings. It's a place you might consider going for a quiet retreat, wandering through the countryside with small, irregular-shaped fields fenced by centuries-old hedgerows and dotted with small thickets of woods.

For me, on that hot August day, marching into Marchefroy at the wrong end of a rifle, the scene before me was anything but peaceful and serene. Sure, I was concerned about myself and my fate. But I was quite certain that I would soon be in a POW camp in the company of fellow flyers who had similar bad luck as I had just an hour before. I was even more concerned about what might happen to those two young men who had tried to help me escape. I knew the Germans did not treat the French who were caught helping flyers with tenderness and respect. The sentence was death for anyone caught helping the enemy. I figured they were goners, and I couldn't help thinking it was my fault.

After I was separated from my two would-be rescuers, the Germans who held me directed me back toward my plane and away from the town. They continued asking about the other crew members and I watched in silence as they searched intently. It was obvious no one could have survived the crash. There was little left of my fighter except a hole in the ground and bits of equipment. It was very close to the house. When I saw how close it was, I was very afraid for anyone who might have been in the house. Tiles from the roof had been blown off from the explosion. A wooden house would likely have exploded into fire, but this house was stone. For an hour they searched and then gave it up. They turned me toward Marchefroy.

It was about a two-kilometer march into the small village. The German soldiers accompanying me asked me no questions, and I attempted no conversation. We entered the town on the road leading from the field and made a right turn toward the center of the groupings of homes and shops. The business end of the rifle kept me steered in the right direction and directly to a building right in the center of the village. I was pushed through the door. It was a small office. My eyes had to adjust to the inside room; one window illuminated it. There was a desk and behind it, an officer. Gestapo. German state police and those responsible for gathering information. I was in for an "interview."

He looked up at me as I came in but he did not stand up. He was older than me, about 30. He did not smile but looked directly at me. I returned his stare. My heart was racing. I was glad I was in uniform, glad I had not taken my 45 pistol. But I knew they could be rough in their search for information, and I steeled myself for what they might dish out. I would not be one who would break. I would stick to the rules, do with me what they might.

"Sit down," the officer ordered in such heavily accented English I had a hard time understanding him.

I sat in the chair facing the desk. He remained sitting. He told me in quite friendly terms that he wanted to find out some information from me about my mission. Would I tell him what I was doing when I was shot down?

"Joseph Frank Moser. First Lieutenant United States Air Corps. 0755999."

He looked at me with a half smile. I couldn't tell if that meant he thought, oh good, this is going to be fun, or if he was just mildly disgusted. But he continued.

"Vhat iss your squadron?" he asked.

"Joseph Frank Moser. First Lieutenant United States Air Corps. 0755999."

"Vhat airplane you fly?"

"Joseph Frank Moser. First Lieutenant United States Air Corps. 0755999."

"Vho iss your base?

"Joseph Frank Moser. First Lieutenant United States Air Corps. 0755999."

With each question the tone became less friendly. But he persisted. He asked where the other crew members were hiding. That was my exception to the questions. I tried to explain that I was the only pilot. I didn't want them spending more time looking for a non-existent flyer and bothering the farmers in the field. Then he returned to the same questions about my unit, my mission, who our commanding officers were, how many were in our unit, what we were trying to attack, and on and on and on.

"Joseph Frank Moser. First Lieutenant United States Air Corps. 0755999." If I repeated it once, I repeated it 50 times. He stopped for a minute and stared at me. There was no hint of friendliness any more. He was angry and frustrated, and the angrier he got the more certain I became that I was only moments away from a beating or far worse. Again I tried to steel myself. I would not give in. I would give them nothing. They could kill me but they would not break me, of that I was as convinced as I could be. But I was awfully scared.

This went on for half an hour, and my interrogator became convinced I would give him nothing useful. He called for the soldiers outside the door who immediately came in—the same soldiers who had marched me in from the field. They spoke fast German, and although it had to do with my fate it was nothing I could understand. One of them motioned with his rifle for me to go out the door, and I was once again in the bright mid-day August sunshine.

We walked only about two blocks before the soldiers pointed me toward a small stone outbuilding attached to a home or barn, I couldn't tell. All the time I was marching in front of them I was continually looking for an opportunity to escape. For some reason, I thought that opportunity would come. I knew if it looked at all feasible, I would make a break for it. Sure, it was risky, but if I wanted to avoid risk I wouldn't have wanted to be a fighter pilot anyway. So when I saw what was to be my prison I quickly scoped out the walls. Heavy stone, about 20 inches thick. We entered through a very heavy wooden door, and I could feel the damp coolness of a cellar. My eyes needed to adjust, but while the door was still open I could see that it was a bare cellar, probably a wine cellar but with no wine or shelves or windows. Just a small room with a dirt floor. Empty except for one garden hoe, and I saw that only for a moment before the door closed behind me and I was in complete darkness.

I heard them latch the door and I thought hopefully I might be able to find a way to jam it open. And then I heard the sound of a heavy motor, a truck no doubt. It came closer to the door until I could tell they had backed it up directly against the door. They didn't want to post a guard there, and they figured that parking a truck against that door would hold me.

I leaned against a wall. The sound of that truck backing against the door discouraged me but only for a moment. Dirt floor, garden hoe. If there was one thing a farm boy from Ferndale, Washington, could do, it was dig. Hah. No stone cellar would keep me for long. I waited, impatiently, but I could hear soldiers outside just beyond the door. I would wait until all was quiet and then dig.

I could hardly stand the wait, I was so eager to accomplish my escape. I imagined walking into our camp at Nueilly near Isigny. Or perhaps riding in on a jeep, driven by an American sergeant after finding me hiding in a ditch or woods by the vanguard of the liberating troops. They would clap me on the back. "Good old Moe!" they would say. "We knew those goons wouldn't be able to hold you down." I'd write a letter to Mom letting her know I'd had a narrow escape but soon I'd finish my 50 missions and would probably come back home to see her and my brother and sisters. I'd be back in a brand new 38, hammering away at my captors. I hoped I'd get a chance to unleash a little ordnance on those guys who took away my two young French friends. But I held back and waited until I thought it might be mid-afternoon, long after I had heard the last of the soldiers outside the door.

I picked up the hoe and I dug. This was no gardening job. I was digging for my life. The dirt flew and sweat started flowing down my face, into my eyes, and down my chest. While much cooler in the cellar than out in the field, it was still warm and I was digging as if my life depended on it. I dug for maybe 15, 20 minutes before pausing to check how I was coming. I felt the footings and I could tell they were deep. Maybe three feet below the floor. I knew how thick the walls were from my quick assessment and I calculated by the progress I made that it would be well into the night before I would have a hole big enough to crawl through. I was grateful for my relatively small size—five foot six inches and all of 155 pounds.

I was thirsty, dreadfully thirsty. It was now mid to late afternoon and I had drank nothing since breakfast. I had dropped into a field, literally feet from death. Had run for my life trying to escape. Had marched in the hot sun, been interrogated and now had dug frantically. All the time experiencing the kind of fear that leaves your mouth dry and an acid taste on your tongue. Nothing I could do about the thirst, except dig. I would find a stream or water from a friendly farmer once I got out.

I had no real idea where I was, and I would have to count on moonlight through the haze to find my way. But I would figure out how to find my way back to the American lines once I got out of this cellar. So I set to digging again, quickly, strongly, steadily. The hole was now almost two feet deep. I figured I had been at it about half an hour, maybe 45 minutes. A few more hours, and I would for sure be under the heavy footings and digging out on the other side of the wall. It was looking good.

Then I heard the sound of voices outside. I froze. The truck next to the door suddenly started up. They were moving the truck! They'd open the door and see my escape attempt. Frantically now I tried to cover the hole with the dirt that had been mounding up next to it. I got down on my knees and pushed the dirt as fast as I could back into the hole. All that work! I heard the truck move away from the door. They'd open it any time. The dirt flew and now I heard them unlatching the door. I jumped up and moved against the wall. The hole was only partially filled in. My heart sank as my hopes for escape disappeared.

The door opened and the bright light nearly blinded me. I could recognize the outline of a German soldier from the ugly helmet shape. And then a man. He was pushed into the cellar. I couldn't see him clearly. I strained, still pushing myself against the back wall. Who was it? Then, another man. The soldier never entered through the door. Never looked in. Never checked to see if I was still there. This was strange.

The heavy wooden door closed again, but now there were two others in the darkness with me. The latch closed again and once again I heard the truck backed up against the door. Now there were three prisoners. Who were they? They might be the young farmers who had tried to help me. I tried to remember their shapes and the quick look I got at these two who entered. But I couldn't be sure. Were they soldiers imprisoned with me to keep me under close watch? I didn't think I could see uniforms, but I couldn't really remember, it had happened so fast.

I said nothing. They said nothing. They did not speak to each other, and so there was no language I could use to determine who they were. I finally decided they had to be placed in here to spy on me, to make certain I wasn't doing anything crazy like trying to dig my way out.

"Shit!" I said quietly to myself alone. I couldn't dig. I saw no chance of escape now. I was stuck in the cellar, getting very hungry and thirstier by the moment. I slid down against the cool stone wall and sat in the pitch darkness. I could hear their breathing and knew they too had settled down against the wall. We would be silent partners in this prison, friend or foe I could not tell. Whether we would share the same fate or if they would be party to mine I could not tell. There was just the quiet breathing of three men in a dark hole.

It was the first time I could think quietly without my mind rattled with thoughts of escape and what might happen in the next moment. I knew now that the morning would tell more than this night possibly could. Whether it was day or night, I had no idea. I just leaned against the wall and thought about this perfectly strange day that had turned my life upside down. Sure, I knew it was possible that something like this might happen. But I never believed it would. Never for a moment. Sitting there in that darkness I still didn't believe it. Was this real? Might I have died? Could this be purgatory? It certainly wasn't heaven, and I couldn't say it was hell either. Had all those things that had happened in the field, running away with the young farmers, capture by the Germans, the fire in my engine, trapped to my plummeting plane by my foot—had all those things really happened? It seemed dreamlike and yet more real than my pitch-black life right now.

I thought about my family. They would get a notice once my unit had decided I was missing. No one had seen me go down. Where was my wingman? Why didn't he go down with me? Suddenly I was angry, and that anger has never completely left me. Why was I left alone in the attack? They could have seen my parachute, known where I was, and could have given my family some hope. Now they would just say I was missing, not certain if I was dead or alive.

I thought about my sisters, Louise and Rosalee. That's what really hurt. I had no girl back home. Hadn't even given much thought to that sort of thing yet. But thinking about my sisters and thinking about the possibility that I might not see them, might not be there for them, might not be the big brother they counted on. That's what hurt in that dark cellar. My little brother Frank, 10 years younger, might have to grow up without a big brother to show him the ropes. And my mother, who had already suffered the loss of her husband, would now lose her oldest son.

I prayed, certainly I did. I prayed the Rosary over and over as I would thousands of times in the days and months ahead. I prayed for those two young men. I prayed for my family, for my friends back at the base who would be worried for me. I prayed for myself, that I would find a way to escape, that I would be strong, that I would be a good airman despite what they might do to me. I prayed that if it was my time to die that I would do so with strength and dignity. And I prayed for food. Oh was I hungry and thirsty.

Finally, I slipped off to sleep. A dark, troubled, uneasy sleep—the sleep of a prisoner. And then I heard the sound of the truck starting up. Suddenly and in an instant I was awake and quickly to my feet. The sound of the latch, and then the door opened with a rusty screech. Light came in, but it was weak and dim. Early morning. A soldier came in holding a rifle, and now through the shadows cast by the ominous shape in the doorway I could see my fellow prisoners. They looked like farmers, Frenchmen. I looked hard—were they the young men who had tried to help me escape? I couldn't tell but they certainly were not Germans. The soldier grabbed them and pushed them through the door. Why were they here? What did they have to do with me? The door closed, and once again I heard the sound of the truck backing up to barricade me in.

I was alone again. I listened intently, listened for a vehicle sound to know if they were driving the prisoners away. Suddenly there was a shot. A rifle shot. Then, another.

Oh my God, I thought. They have been shot. I slumped down against the wall and felt that I was going to throw up. I felt as if the shot had gone into my own gut, or that someone had kicked me. There was no doubt in my mind about what had happened. They had simply lined these two young men up and shot them. Late twenties, maybe older, maybe younger, I didn't really get a good look. But two men had died because I had the stupidity to get shot down. Two men who had spent that quiet night with me in that cellar had died because they had tried to help me. We could have dug out. Why didn't I try to find out who they were and why they were there? We could have dug out. We could have escaped together. Now, I could picture them, lying against the wall of one of those homes I had walked by yesterday, blood staining the dirt, eyes open.

And I knew something else now. If this is what these bastards would do to two young French men, probably farmers from the field who tried to help me, what would they do to me, someone who yesterday had been flying big guns and bombs around trying to kill them? What was my life worth? There was no thought of escape now. Only fear of what would happen when they opened that door for me.

04 FRESNES PRISON

I had about 45 minutes to an hour to think about what would happen to me when the Germans again opened the door. My hunger and thirst were gone, replaced by a painful vice grip in my gut. Then I heard the truck starting up again and I knew it was my turn. An hour in the pitch darkness to agonize over the killing of those two French men who died because they were brave enough or foolish enough to try and help an American flyer stay out of German hands. I cannot tell you now if my dread and sick feeling was more for them or for the almost certain fate that awaited me just beyond that door. All I know is that I was more scared than I had ever been. More scared then when running away and expecting a bullet in the back. More scared than when bailing out of my burning plane. More scared than when I realized my trapped foot had nearly brought me into the middle of that explosion.

The heavy wooden door was unlatched and creaked open. The German soldier's silhouette appeared and looked into the dark cellar to see where I was. He grabbed me, rifle in one hand; not roughly, just firmly as if he was in complete command, which he was. I was pushed into the bright August morning sunlight, half expecting to see my executioner's rifle leveled against my chest. Instead, I saw a black car waiting. Without any explanation, I was pushed in. I did not even have time to look around and see where they might have executed my fellow prisoners or buried them in the short time since they were taken from the cellar.

In the back seat of the black sedan, a German soldier sat next to me with a rifle leveled at me at all times. The driver pulled out sharply, and so I left Marchefroy behind. But the sickening dread of what havoc my crash had left in the lives of the brave French villagers of Marchefroy never left me. That is, until 1988.

Many years after the war I began to get involved in POW groups. One was the rather exclusive KLB — the Konzentration Lager Buchenwald association (lager means camp in German). This was a group for survivors of the Buchenwald concentration camp. At one of the POW meetings that I attended in Seattle, I reconnected with Jim Hastin, who had become my best friend while on the train ride from the prison in Paris to Buchenwald. Jim's P-51 went down in flames while on a strafing run in May, 1944, and he had bailed out near the town of Anet, less than five miles from Marchefroy. After his retirement Jim moved back to his hometown, which was only about an hour away from where I lived. The town is a picturesque seaside community called Anacortes and is right on Northern Puget Sound, so we had many opportunities to get together. In Buchenwald I also met Art Kinnis, a Canadian flying as navigator on a Lancaster bomber for the Royal Air Force, who had been shot down only a half mile from where my P-38 crashed. After the war, Art returned to his home in Victoria, British Columbia, Canada, only a few hours away by ferry ride and less than 40 miles as the crow flies from my home in Ferndale.

By 1988, these two gentlemen had both become officers of the KLB. Art was the president, and Jim was the treasurer. They got together frequently to work on KLB business, which was usually focused on trying to find what happened to the survivors of Buchenwald and getting in touch with them. On a very memorable day in 1988, the two of them were working together at Art's home in Victoria. While going through Art's papers, they came across a letter addressed to Art, from Francois Vermeulen, written in November, 1945. Francois had written this to Art because he and his wife, Jacqueline, had hidden Art in their farmhouse for several weeks to keep him out of German hands and help him get back to England. He had developed a strong bond with the Vermeulen family, which exists to this day. The letter, sadly, had been misplaced and was never translated. So when Jim and Art discovered it, they took the letter into the library in Victoria to find someone who could translate it for them. Once they had the letter translated, they read it to me over the phone.

In the letter, Francois explained what happened in the village after the war and told of some of his and his family's courageous underground activities. He then told the story of the attempted rescue of the American "captain" who crashed near their house. The "captain" was me. I found out that Francois was one of the farmers in the field and that he was the one who had more or less taken command. It was Francois' brother, Leon, who had been one of the two young men who had tried to help me get to the woods before the Germans captured us. I also found out that the prisoners in the cellar with me were farmers from the field. One most certainly was Henri Eustache, the mayor of Marchefroy. The other was most likely Leon. It was clear from the letter that, while my plane crashed very near that farmhouse, no one was injured or killed.

Not all of these details were in Francois' letter. Many were provided during the writing of this book by a wonderfully helpful school teacher in France by the name of Remco Immerzeel. Remco has made it his hobby and passion to learn the details about the capture and fate of the Allied flyers who ended up in Buchenwald. It was through Remco that I found some amazing details of the story of my capture and the fate of the brave resistance fighters and farmers who were helping me.

Through interviews with the Vermeulen family and other farmers who were in the field that day — such as Mr. Rene Saillard — Remco was able to piece together a fairly complete picture of what had happened on the 13th of August following my crash.

Several of the farmers were arrested by the Germans after my capture and taken to Bercheres, a village southeast of Marchefroy on the main road. Bercheres is where the German Werhmacht, or Army commander of the area, had his headquarters. There they were interrogated, and some of them were let go because they did not have information. Those arrested included Rene Saillard, two others named LeDuc and DeCeranno. Francois had escaped the Germans, made a run for it and hid out for some time about 25 miles away. Leon and Henri Eustache were returned to Marchefroy and put in the cellar with me. Most likely, this was because they were most directly involved in my attempted escape, and the cellar was the most secure holding cell the Germans had.

Reading the translated letter from Francois made it clear that the two in the cellar with me had not been killed. But it took another nearly 20 years after discovering that letter to find out how they escaped. One of the German soldiers involved in my capture and in the arrest of the French fieldworkers was a Frenchman himself from Alsace. He went by the name of Paul

Renaud and had been pressed into the German army, serving as a French translator. He was the Kommandant's sidecar driver, and it is quite possible that he was the one driving the sidecar through the field when I was caught. Although in German uniform, he did all he could do in his power to help his native country, including supporting the resistance activities. After helping secure the release or escape of some of the French farmers who had been taken to Bercheres, he was assigned to go and get the two men out of the cellar that morning. Instead of returning them to his fellow soldiers, he told them to run for it and then fired two shots in the air to make it sound as if he had tried to foil their escape.

After the war, Mr. Renaud was a very popular man in the area because the French villagers were very aware of his heroism in helping the French cause. He married a local woman, ran a gas station in one of the villages nearby and died in the mid-1990s.

While many of these details came later, when I heard Jim Hastin reading Francois' letter to me over the phone in 1988, my life changed forever. I felt weak in the knees, and a heavy burden that I had carried for 44 years was lifted. My crash had not resulted in any injuries or deaths. The brave men and women did not suffer because of my unwelcome arrival in their oat field. The nightmares that plagued me all the years after the war finally stopped and did not return. It seemed the last fetter the Germans had placed on me dropped away and I was free.

But that was all in the future. For now, I rode in that hot, black car and stared at the end of a rifle held in my face. I'm sure the scenery was pretty, but I wasn't paying attention to that. I guessed we were heading to Paris. That is where the German strength was and also where Gestapo headquarters was located. Besides, the villages were getting closer together, and soon there were signs of a large city. This was not how I wanted to visit this famous city. I had seen Paris from the air many times, but I had always assumed I would be enjoying it as a tourist. This clearly was not going to be a quiet, peaceful visit to the City of Lights. We pulled onto a broad boulevard lined with trees and then swerved sharply to drive through an archway into a brick courtyard of a handsome, ornate building covered with large Nazi flags. The car came to a quick stop, and the door was opened by a grim-faced soldier. Gestapo headquarters, no doubt. Again, I could taste the fear in my mouth. The questioning I had in the quiet village of Marchefroy would likely seem a mere chat with my buddies compared to what was to come next.

I barely had time to look around the courtyard before being ushered through the tall, ornately carved doors. We climbed the stairs facing the entrance, and our footsteps echoed along with the conversations of German officers who were walking through the massive halls. I was pushed through a door and entered a very large, very impressive office. There were lots of windows, paneled walls, a massive desk and one very stiff German officer sitting behind the desk reading some papers. The soldier accompanying me brought me right in front of him, and I stood there. He looked up. He had an immaculate uniform with enough decoration on it to communicate that he was an experienced, high-ranking officer. He was about 30 years old with blond hair and was very handsome. His English was considerably better than my inquisitor in Marchefroy.

"Lieutenant Moser," he said, casually and with a slight smile. "We would like to know the names of the men in your airplane."

I wanted to say, look you ignorant goon, don't you know what a P-38 is? There's only one pilot and that was me! But I didn't.

"Joseph Frank Moser. First Lieutenant United States Air Corps. 0755999." I said it quietly and firmly. He stared at me and smiled. I tried to read his expression. This man could order my execution in a moment, or perhaps have me beat either to death or until I broke. But I would give him nothing more. A slight smile cornered his lips but I couldn't tell if it meant you poor bastard, wait until you see what's in store for you, or if it was a sign of recognition of a military man of dignity. It didn't matter.

"What unit are you in?"

"Joseph Frank Moser. First Lieutenant United States Air Corps. 0755999."

"What's your commanding officer's name?"

"Joseph Frank Moser. First Lieutenant United States Air Corps. 0755999."

He stood up and I could tell there was anger boiling beneath his disciplined face. I felt my knees knocking. He was a big man and no doubt had done his share of the rougher forms of interrogation. I was sure at any minute he would come around the desk or bark an order to the soldiers standing outside the door. Instead, he kept asking questions.

For two hours this went on. He became angry and frustrated, but never stopped the questions. He sat down and was quiet for a bit. Then he looked at me with that enigmatic smile and said.

"Joe, you come from a town called Bellingham in Washington State. Your mother's name is Mary. You were promoted to First Lieutenant on July 10, 1944. Congratulations. Apparently you've been doing some pretty good flying. You fly with the 429th Fighter Squadron of the 474th Fighter Group. You fly out of a temporary base in France called Nueilly right near Isigny."

My mouth dropped open.

"Your fellow pilots include Lieutenants Nolby, Lane, Cobb, Patterson, Mills, Skiles, Schwarzrock and Hazzard. You want me to name more? Your commanding officer is Major Burl Glass. Shall I go on?"

I stared in complete disbelief. He proceeded to tell me more about my buddies, unit and missions than even I knew. It shook me more than a fist to the solar plexus, and for a minute I wasn't sure if my knees would hold me. What didn't this guy know? How did they know all of this? Was there a spy in our unit? Had they tortured captured pilots to get this information?

"Oh yes, George Knox, he was shot down on 23 May, right? He's a POW. Don't worry, he's doing fine."

Now I was shook up, and he could tell. I was sweating profusely, but stayed at attention. What about Captain Larson, I wanted to ask. What can you tell me about him? But I didn't say anything. My back was hurting and I was terribly thirsty — and hungry.

"So Joe, help yourself out here a little bit. I just want to know that you are going to be helpful. Tell me what your orders where on 13 August — what was your target?"

I hesitated. What was the point of this? They knew more than I could tell them. Nothing I could offer would add to their information. Then I answered: "Joseph Frank Moser. First Lieutenant United States Air Corps. 0755999."

And then it was over. He called for the guard who quickly entered, spun me around and took me from the interrogators office. I was confused, upset and for some strange reason, somehow, I felt I had given them something. I was disoriented and angry.

I don't really remember the car ride to the prison. I was relieved that the interrogation was over and that I had at least for now avoided a vicious beating or worse. But I was getting weak from lack of fluid and food. It was now about noon, and no one had offered me anything to eat or drink. And I didn't ask.

We pulled into another big archway into another courtyard, but it was clear that this was not some ornate hotel or office building that had been commandeered by the Germans. This was a prison — dark, ugly and foreboding. Small windows circled around the courtyard. It was the famous French prison called Fresnes. With 1200 dingy cells, it was well known before and after the war as France's toughest prison.

There were two massive wooden doors at the entrance, and they were opened to let me in. I immediately was sent down a hallway to the right. The hallway was incredibly long and dark, lit with an occasional bulb — enough to see with but dim enough to make the hallway look like a tunnel leading to a tomb. The walk down the hallway was short. The guard opened up a cell door near the entrance, and I was escorted in. Clearly, they knew where I was supposed to go. My arrival was planned.

It was dark and mercifully cooler in the tiny cell. The door slammed and locked behind me. I was alone. My eyes adjusted to the dim light, and I could see a concrete bed on one wall, covered with a dirty and very thin straw mattress. There was no toilet, only a hole in the floor and a small concrete sink. Cold water. I drank deep, and for a moment felt like I might still be alive. I splashed the water on my hot face and breathed deeply with my eyes closed, hands propping me up against the sink and my head drooping down. Yes, I was alive — weak, tired, afraid, terribly alone — but alive.

My thirst finally quenched, I sat down on the bed. I felt the thin, filthy mattress. Looking around the cell I noticed a small window up near the very high ceiling; there were bars on it. A little light was coming through the dirty glass, and I was grateful for that. I laid down and felt the hard concrete right through the mattress. I did not notice until after leaving the cell how many "friends" shared this cell and mattress with me — the place was literally crawling with bugs. Like everyone else who experienced the delights of Fresnes, I carried with me the scars of those bug bites forever. But, as I laid down, my thoughts were not on fighting bugs or even fighting Germans.

It was the first time I had been alone for any length of time since my capture. The two hours of digging frantically in the cellar didn't count because I had hope of escape. There was no hope here. My fate was completely in the hands of an enemy who had demonstrated to me, through what I thought was the murder of those two Frenchmen, that they were without humanity or mercy. No, I decided, my fate is not in their hands. I fingered the Rosary in my mind and felt some moments of a deep sadness that felt almost like peace.

How would mother deal with the news? Would they tell her I was dead? No one had seen me go down. I was MIA. I choked up thinking about her getting the dreaded envelope. At least with that telegram there would be some hope. Keep hoping, Mom. Keep hoping and praying as I know you are.

My dear sweet sisters. And little brother Frank. I had always dreamed of being a fighter pilot. Ever since I saw that story about the new P-38 while in high school, all I had thought about was learning to fly that marvelous machine. I thought about shooting others out of the sky, about coming home a hero, about telling my brother and my sisters how I made them proud during the war. Now, I would have done anything to be home again. This part of it just wasn't in the plan. Sure, I knew something bad could happen. But it wouldn't, not to me. I was brave, a good pilot. I would come home. Mom was working at Safeway now. She couldn't work the farm by herself and had sold it in '42. Louise, 18 now, practically grown up and thinking about boys all the time. And sweet, sweet Rosalee. Little Frank — he needed a big brother at home to show him the way. Dear Mother, let me see them all again. Please! I wondered what time it was back home. I tried to think about what they were doing, when they would get the telegram, what they would think.

In the meantime, the fleas were feasting. I dropped off to a tear-stained sleep.

Translated copy of Francois Vermeulen's letter to Art Kinnis
(November, 1945) First translated 1988

I was really glad to receive your news and to know that you are safe and in good health. I think of your wounds that you had while hiding. I have asked myself what you thought of us while you were trapped in that camp. If your friends had not arrived we would have joined you at Buchenwald.

Now I will tell you what happened after you left. We thought that you had arrived home and now I see that the opposite was the case (by your letter) a large deception for me.

In July we again did some nice work because we blew up a railway bridge and also there were about 50 goons [German soldiers] who died and the railway was completely out of order until the end of hostilities; and after we received an order to destroy a tunnel and a munition train at the same time but sadly were short of ammunition. After that we were occupied by the Germans and bombs were coming from all corners and also airplanes.

An every day occurrence until August 13th at 10 o'clock we saw an allied airplane in flames the pilot who was an American captain jumped from the burning Lightning. Pilot and plane fell 800 m from your Lancaster. Immediately I joined the captain in questions and gave him one of my shirts, a cap and sweater and all that in a few minutes; [note: Joe is certain he remained in uniform — an important point relating to POW status] we were passing the German barrage for they were in every corner. I told the captain, always with me, to take my brother's directions who was working in a field. That was around 600 m from where he fell. The Germans knowing what happened arrived in a sidecar made him and my brother prisoners and threatened them with execution if they didn't give information about other pilots. The Germans 3 in each sidecar had spread out and looked all over the fields to find some other aviators.

While that was happening my brother evaded and was obliged to hide himself and I did also.

I left the backyard of the farm while some other Germans SS were

*coming in to take my brother and the farmhands to hold for ransom.
They took 2 from the farm, the mayor that you know very well and also
2 others**. They kept them for 24 hours without food or water telling
them that they would be executed.*

*I left home for 2 days and when I came back 15th Aug I was forced to
hide myself in a tree and shrubs the whole afternoon because I did not
wish to be caught by the Germans because in their retreat they were
taking men, horses, carriages to carry their luggage. 16th and 17th Aug
was a (indecipherable) but on the 18th at 15 hours they all returned
and at the same time we felt at liberty in movement and speech and at
last a joy that can't be described.*

*As for your bad departure we are working on it and the man that gave
you away will have an accident during the last bombardment. As soon
as I have more details I will send them to you.*

*I have to tell you that you were mistaken, it is that my parents and also
Paulette's parents where you were because Paulette and Maurice were
at Evereux.*

*As for Andre he is in good health and came out safe from his torture. If
you remember well he didn't have any news of his wife that the Germans
had imprisoned. She was at Fresnes on 17th August and the 18th she
was to have been executed but the advancing Allies opened the prison
doors. She was able to go back to her home around the end of August.*

*Other news of my wife Jacqueline. She gave birth to a nice big son 10
Nov 1944 that we baptized Jean Bernard. In 2 days he will be 9 months
old and already is a little devil.*

*I will also give you my new address because I hope that we will receive
some of your news. It will please me very much.*

*If one day you anticipate returning to France do not forget to visit us. I
will see you with pleasure. Write soon. Please receive from my wife and
self our good friendships for your wife and self and big kisses for your
little girl. If you can send me a little tobacco and chocolate it will give us
much pleasure for we are very restricted.*

Francois Vermeulen

05 THE TRAIN

"Raus! Raus!"

It was eight or nine in the morning. I had woken earlier from an uneasy, flea-bitten sleep in the most notorious prison in all of France: Fresnes. I could hear sounds of cell doors being unlocked and prisoners talking over the shouts of the German guards. Since I was only in Fresnes one night, I couldn't know how unusual this was. Many others had been in this depressing and frightful place for a long time, and they knew better than I that the sound of cell doors opening would usually lead to the sound of the firing squad outside. For me, however, it was a welcome sound. Perhaps food, perhaps exercise.

As I heard the sound of the cell doors opening closer and closer to me, I also noticed a distant rumbling. Thunder? No, it looked too light through my small window high up on the wall to be stormy outside. Could it be shelling? The continual rolling sound made it clear. The Allies were close enough that distant sound of artillery could be heard. It cheered me, but for the French resistance fighters who made up the bulk of the inmates, that was a frightening sound. They were all but certain that as the Allies closed in, their days would be numbered. The Germans certainly would not just walk away and let the Allies open the prison doors.

"Raus!" They shouted. "Get out! Get out!" Now the shouting and clanging was just outside my door.

Now what? I thought. What new horrors might this day unveil? Maybe it will bring good news. Hopefully, get out of this hell hole of a cell and get to a POW camp. Join my fellow flyers, receive some Red Cross packages and start to be treated like a captured combatant rather than a common criminal. I had no idea at the time just what was going on in this horrible place and in the stirred city outside. Hitler had replaced the top commander of Gross Paris, or greater Paris, with General Dietrich von Choltitz, a hardened battle commander who had led the German army during the siege of Sebastapol. Before heading to Paris to take up his new command, von Choltitz met with the Führer, who made it clear that von Choltitz was to fight in the streets of Paris to the last man and, if defeated, to leave the city a wasteland. The new commander was well known for his unerring loyalty to the Nazi cause, and Hitler had every reason to believe that von Choltitz would make sure that not a brick of the most beautiful city in the world would be left in one piece.

Both sides in the conflict were aware of what happened in Warsaw, Poland, as the Russian armies advanced. The people rose up against the hated occupiers, and a bloodbath ensued, leaving hundreds of thousands dead and a city largely ruined. The same fate was awaiting Paris, particularly if the Resistance were to lead a wholesale uprising of the population — many of whom were eagerly waiting for the signal "Aux Barricades!"

It was now August 15 — two days after I bailed out of my plane — and this was the day the officials and citizens of Paris began openly defying their German occupiers. The Metro workers, Gendarmerie (military police) and police all went on strike. The strike was actually ordered by the Communist wing of the Resistance, which was in a life and death battle with the French resistance fighters that were loyal to General de Gaulle, the leader of Free France. The first sign of general uprising was followed by a general strike of the entire city on August 18, with open battles between armed resistance fighters and the occupiers. Behind the scenes, both sides of the Resistance were fighting to take control, and Eisenhower — who had decided to avoid Paris — was forced to march on the city with French General LeClerc in the lead. On August 25, the Allies entered Paris and the next day the famous Champs-Elysees boulevard was the scene of the first victory parade.

At the time, I had no idea that I was an eyewitness — with a very limited view — of some of the most gripping and dramatic moments of the war. I just wanted out of the hateful place. The Germans were intent that the 3500 prisoners held in Fresnes would not be liberated. So as the Allies approached, and the unrest in the streets started turning into open battles, the executions intensified. And now, just a day after I arrived, they were evacuating most of the prison, starting with the order "Raus!"

I heard the jangle of keys outside my door and it was flung open. I could see prisoners outside and I quickly joined the crowd in the long, dark corridor. Almost immediately I saw a familiar and incredibly welcome face.

"Captain Larson!" I shouted.

"Lieutenant!" He called with as much surprise and delight as I felt. Now I'm not the huggy type, but we embraced, and to this day I can still recall the feeling of joy, comfort and relief in seeing not just a familiar face, but the face of a leader whom I deeply respected. Suddenly, the world felt a different place despite the circumstances. For some reason, with Captain Larson there was hope, and hope is one of those few things that are needed in even the most desperate circumstances.

"What are you doing here?" we both asked each other at exactly the same moment. I wanted desperately to find out what had happened to him. We hadn't heard a word from him since he had been shot down in June — just a few weeks earlier. He was our squadron leader, and things hadn't been the same without him. He was a genuine hero to us and a real veteran, having fought in the air war in North Africa in '42, shooting down several enemy planes. He was the only one in our unit to have been shot down twice. In North Africa he had eluded capture and returned to fly again and lead us with his courage and skill. We hoped that he had escaped twice, but now I knew this time he had not been so lucky. Unfortunately, there was practically no time to talk. The Germans were in a hurry and they were herding the prisoners down the crowded corridor toward the main entrance. We were pushed and jostled until we once again emerged into the big courtyard in front of the heavy entrance doors.

As my eyes adjusted to the light and scanned the gathering crowd, I could see that most of the prisoners were French men, with some women mixed in. I could also see that I was not the only American. In fact, I would soon find there were 168 Allied flyers in the courtyard along with almost 2500 French men and women. In Fresnes there had been 803 French women in total, and 400 of them along with 2104 men — including us — had been selected for the ride out. Fresnes was primarily where the Germans held captured French resistance fighters before they were sent on trains to concentration camps deep in Germany. Most never returned. In fact, of the more than 2500 French men and women who stood in the August morning sunshine that day, only about 300 returned to France.

Almost all of the 168 Allied flyers in the courtyard that day had been captured while in the hands of the French Resistance. I was in that group too, even though it could hardly be said that I was in the Resistance's hands. Altogether we would find out that there were 48 Royal Air Force (British) flyers, 82 American flyers, 26 Royal Canadian Air Force flyers, two New Zealanders, nine Australians and one Jamaican. Almost all of them had been betrayed by one man and his red-headed girlfriend, who had successfully infiltrated five major resistance cells. Those betrayed included my good friends Art Kinnis and Jim Hastin. I was one of the few who had not been betrayed but who had been caught with those trying to help me escape. So we were all in the same boat. In German eyes, we were not just captured combatants, but a part of the Resistance effort that had caused them so much trouble, death, inconvenience and frustration. Being caught up in the web of betrayed French Resistance was the real source of our troubles — the result of which would soon become painfully clear. To the Germans, the Resistance fighters were terrorists, not enemy combatants. And because we were caught with them, we too were considered terrorists and were actually given the official designation "terrorfliegers," or terrorist flyers.

While 2500 of us had been released from our cells and were getting organized for the trip out, there were over 500 prisoners still left in their cells. There is little doubt that the reason they were left is that the Gestapo intended to execute them at Fresnes before the Allies arrived. Indeed, that is what the prisoners themselves expected. Instead, according to the book, *Is Paris Burning*, they survived and were liberated through the extraordinary efforts of the Swedish Consul officer Raoul Nordling with invaluable assistance from a German counter-intelligence officer Emil "Bobby" Bender.

While we were focused on trying to find our flying buddies, the Germans were trying to get us organized for the journey ahead. I had no idea where we were going, and neither did Captain Larson. We assumed again it was to a POW camp, which would be none too soon as far as I was concerned. I didn't like the looks of these Gestapo guards one bit. We should be in the hands of the Luftwaffe. An assortment of trucks and buses appeared outside the big archway leading to the street and outside world. Soon we were boarding these vehicles, all jumbled together without any order and closely guarded by well-armed Gestapo officers.

Personally, I don't remember the ride, but I do remember marching to the train station. I recall it being about a two- to three-hour march in the hot sun, closely guarded all the time. But it finally gave us the opportunity to start meeting our fellow prisoners and to learn how we all ended up in this particularly desperate situation. If one had to be in these conditions, it was at least made inestimably better by the company of fellows bound by training, experience and values. Misery, indeed, loves company.

It was hot, and the August sun was now beating down on us mercilessly from overhead. It was early afternoon, and the air was heavy with humidity. We arrived at the Pantin freight yard, northeast of a main train station, Gare l'Est. Pantin is adjacent to the Paris stockyards and I would soon find out that this was no coincidence. When we got to the train station, I could see we were in a large freight yard. I saw two tracks and there in front of us was a long train — not of passenger cars, but cattle cars. I looked at them for a moment. This was to be our transportation? How long would it take to get to the POW camp? This could not be pleasant. I would soon find out that "unpleasant" would not describe it.

Art Kinnis recalls that before boarding we were given food. He says one loaf of bread, a box of knackerbread and a tin of horse meat. This, he was told, was for six prisoners and would last the two to seven days of the journey. Jim Hastin also recalls getting food. I do not. I just remember being very, very hungry.

In the freight yard, our guards worked to achieve some semblance of order. For the first time, our group of airmen was more or less brought together. We would be loaded into cars as a group — two cars for the lot of us, with a few Frenchmen mixed in with us. The French resistance fighters had been separated into groups of men and women, and the women had been the first to be taken to the rail yard. Then the loading began. The cars were marked 40/8. That meant they were intended to carry up to 40 men or 8 cattle. Forty men would have been a fairly tight fit. The 95 they put into our car was more than inhuman. If I felt uneasy about the looks of these cattle cars, I became almost panicky as they began pushing me into a car already overloaded with fellow prisoners.

I found myself near the middle of the car. At least I was in the company of fellow airmen, including many Americans. But instantly it was unbearably hot and when the big doors were pushed closed and bolted down with a metallic clank, the air quickly disappeared, filled instead with the odor of 95 men, complete strangers to each other who were now nose to nose, arm to arm, leg to leg. It was immediately obvious that I was not the only one who had not bathed in days. In fact, I guess that because of my comparatively very short stay in Fresnes and the fact that only three days prior I had taken a shower in my own rustic base, I was probably one of the cleanest on that train — and that wasn't saying much. The only ventilation was provided by openings about one foot high and three feet wide near the top and at each end of the car. Barbed wire was stretched across these small openings to discourage anyone from thinking they might fit through. Two five-gallon buckets had been pushed into the car with us. One had water and it was to be our water supply. The other was empty, and it would be our toilet. It would only be a few minutes before the incredible stench of 95 hot, unwashed bodies was blended with the even greater stench of the urine and excrement that quickly accumulated and then overflowed from that bucket. The problem of simply squeezing through that press of dirty men to get to the bucket was enough of a problem; then to find it overflowing and sloshing about against the men unfortunate enough to have to stand near it was, well, sickening.

I heard the train engine roar louder and started hearing the distinctive sound of the train cars being jerked as the slack in the couplings was taken up one by one, a loud bang accompanying each violent start. Our car was in the front third of the train. Suddenly, there was a sharp jerk as our car was caught up in the acceleration, bodies pushed against each other even tighter, curses, shoves, apologies and pushing against each other for balance. Our journey began. We had no idea how long this extreme misery would last. We only had the very reasonable expectation that whatever would come next would be better than this. Reasonable, but wrong.

There was little opportunity to move around. The bodies were so close that normal conversation felt awkward. But it wasn't long before I heard a strong voice and saw that it belonged to someone standing near me. A big, blond man with an engaging smile and obvious charisma. It didn't take long before I heard he was from Victoria, B.C., a navigator for the Royal Air Force, shot down in a Lancaster bomber right near the location I was shot down, only many weeks earlier. It was Art Kinnis, and a friendship that lasts to this day was started.

Then I picked up on another conversation. This was coming from the front of the car. I struggled to get a little closer. I thought I heard the name of a familiar town. I got close enough to see who was talking. Another good-sized guy (of course, being all of five feet six inches in height, most of the guys seemed pretty big to me). He had light brown hair and seemed a very pleasant fellow.

"Did I hear you say you were from Anacortes?" I said.

"Yeah," he answered. "Anacortes, Washington. Way up by the islands, not far from Canada."

"Yeah, I know where it is," I said. "I'm from Ferndale."

"Ferndale, Washington?" he said with a laugh. "That's practically in my back yard."

"Yep," I said. "My name is Joe. Joe Moser."

"I'm Jim Hastin," he said, and so I met my closest buddy during the horrible experiences ahead and someone who became one of my closest friends years later, in the 1980s, when we met again at a POW meeting in Seattle. Jim was simply one of the best friends any guy could have.

"How'd you get here?" I asked. It was the standard question now. We all had stories to tell and wanted to hear each other's as well.

"I shot myself down," he said with a wry smile. "Flying a P-51, I blew up a train that had a little more ammunition on it than I figured. The fireball lit my engine on fire and I bailed."

By this time we were sitting down on our haunches. It was the only way we could get any rest from the endless standing, but only a few could do it at a time. After awhile, we even gave up this strategy and we all ended up just falling down on each other, two and three deep.

"Well, I ran into a little anti-aircraft fire. Lost my left engine on my P-38."

"You got two engines on those planes. You couldn't get back?"

"Fire," I said. "It got too hot and I had to bail just a few miles from our lines."

"Where was that?" he asked.

"North of Houdan," I said. "Bailed out near Marchefroy."

"You got to be kidding me," he said. "I came out close to Anet. That's only about three miles from there."

It wasn't long before we found out that Art also came from the same neck of the woods as we did and that he also had crashed in the same area as Jim and I did. In fact, Art's crash site was almost exactly the same as mine — near a farm called Les Gatins des Oulins. We shared a home territory, we shared similar ends to our careers as airmen and now we were sharing the same fate — not just of being captured by enemies, but of being evaders and a part of the hated French Resistance. We were designated not just enemy flyers by Hitler and his thugs, but we were labeled "terrorfliegers," terrorists deserving not of Geneva Convention protection, but of concentration camp and execution. We didn't know it at the time — ignorance is bliss sometimes, but we did know that the misery we were now enduring we would endure together. And there was some small comfort in that.

We would have taken comfort in something else if we had known it was happening. We had not been abandoned when leaving Paris. The Resistance fighters in Paris were very well aware of our departure, as our train carried many of the Resistance leaders and family members of those still in the city actively engaged in undermining the occupiers. In fact, on the train was the leader of the Resistance fighters in Paris, Pierre Lefaucheux, who had been arrested on June 7. His wife, on hearing that Fresnes had been emptied of prisoners, jumped on her bicycle and followed the train outside the city. She followed it for miles and miles. Remarkably, this incredible woman later successfully got her husband released from Buchenwald. The Resistance was not about to let all their fighters, leaders and family members disappear without a fight. Once it was determined which rail line the prisoners' train was on, the order went out to stop the train and rescue the passengers.

Back in the Pantin freight yard, while we were loaded and waiting in the sweltering heat of the cattle cars for our journey to start, a teenaged boy was frantically pedaling his bicycle to the village of Nanteuil-Saacy. He carried an oral order to the leader of the Resistance in this village: "Cut the rail line from Paris to Nancy — at any cost." And this message was sent by coded radio to London: "Germans ordered organized evacuation detainees Paris prisons particularly Fresnes by rail via Metz Nancy. Fear general massacre during trip. Take all measures possible sabotage transport."

The effort was underway to rescue us, but we had no idea at the time. And such a rescue could be as dangerous to those they intend to rescue as to the attackers and guards.

06 CATTLE CAR TO HELL

In the first hours of that train ride out of Paris — the last train out of Paris before the city was liberated — we found out how well we had done in disrupting French transportation infrastructure. Everywhere along the route were disruptions from the strafing, bombing and efforts of the Resistance. The train ride was not one smooth journey from Paris to Germany, but a constant series of stops, starts, jerks, waiting and starting up again. All the time we were jammed together into a filthy, sweaty, fearful mass of humanity. Every stop and jerking startup shoved us into each other all over again, jarring nerves and threatening what little sense of brotherhood we had together. Hatred and anger germinate quickly in such conditions. This was the enemy we were fighting, this was the enemy's way. This was the respect they showed to their fellow human beings. If we ever had the chance to go up in our beautiful flying weapons again, we would do so with so much more meaning, determination and animosity.

During one of the frequent stops in the few miles outside of Paris, we were allowed out of the cars. It was hours into our ride, and the one five-gallon bucket had quickly filled and overflowed so we were allowed to relieve ourselves alongside the tracks. Though I did not see the cars of women who were also let out, others who witnessed said they had stripped to their underwear because of the heat and crowded conditions and were forced to answer nature's call in the same way men were. At first, it was humiliating and shameful. But we quickly became desensitized, and in the days ahead it was just one more part of our life. Every moment was an experience in degradation and horror — urinating or defecating in these conditions was just one more of many.

Meanwhile, the Resistance was determined to do all they could to stop what they were certain would be a massacre of their fellow patriots, friends and family members. The few brave members of the Resistance quickly did the necessary job in the cover of the evening darkness — with precious explosives they had received either from Allied air drops or through stealing from the occupiers, they nearly destroyed the railroad bridge over the Marne river. But there were only a few of them, and they had neither the weapons nor the manpower to overwhelm the guards charged with bringing us into the dark heart of Germany. So they waited, impatiently no doubt, for reinforcements to arrive from Paris or the surrounding villages.

We had no idea, of course, that this rescue effort was going on. But we knew something was up. Nighttime came with halting, jerking progress, and we pulled into a long tunnel. Before emerging from the other end we came to a metal-grinding, squealing stop. Now what, we wondered?

In the pitch dark we stood quietly on the tracks with the shouts of the guards around us. We could hear them running around barking orders and answering each other's questions. In just a few minutes a new terror and threat to our fragile lives emerged. The train's big engine kept running, quickly filling the tunnel with clouds of thick, black smoke. The tunnel, which was already unbearably hot and virtually airless, became impossible to breathe in, and we started coughing and wheezing, taking in big gulps of the fouled air to try to get enough oxygen into our bodies. Cries of anguish and fear from the frightened passengers mingled with the shouts from the guards.

"We're going to die here!" some shouted as if the SS guards could care about that. I tilted my head back, fighting between keeping the thick smoke out of my lungs and trying to pull in what little useful air was available. It kept getting thicker and hotter and more frightening. I looked at the faces around me and saw fear and panic. No, I thought, I didn't come all the way from the farm in Ferndale, all the way through flight school, survive 43 missions over enemy territory, get shot down just to die of suffocation in some stupid French tunnel. Yet my lungs told me that unless my fellow passengers and I got some air soon we would indeed die. Again I prayed, thinking of my family, a future taken from me, the sorrow of those who loved me. Tears from the stinging smoke were running down our faces, mixing with the sweat that still poured from us, greasing our unwelcome contact with each other. Now the cars did sound like cattle cars on the way to the slaughter house with bawling and crying and screaming and curses. A few began to collapse and those around them tried to make just a bit more room so they had a path to what little air was above them. I kept quiet, but my head was spinning as I kept coughing and sucking in that black death.

Nearly two hours of fear, panic and suffocation later, we heard the doors of cars near us pushed open on the metal slides. Shouts of panic were mixed with urgent and hopeful cries: "Get out!" "Hurry!" "Push!" Soon our door slid open and the men in our car began to pile out, falling, gasping, tumbling, yelling. The tunnel was filled with the black smoke, making the darkness palpable. Once out, we could immediately sense that there was more air now that we were on the ground and not contained in the 40 by 8.

Guards were shouting orders again, and we were led back toward the entrance of the tunnel. We walked as quickly as we could — each step taking us closer to clean, un-fouled air. Finally, we came out into the dark of midnight or early morning and sucked into our tortured lungs that rich air of the French countryside. Everywhere there was coughing and moaning, but the horrible panic was gone. We could at least breathe.

We had no idea what had halted our progress through the tunnel. Years later we would hear from a fellow Allied flyer, John Watson, who also lived near Art and myself in Surrey, British Columbia. He had been on a passenger train that left Paris about the same time our freight train did. His train was behind ours and had stopped just outside the tunnel entrance while we were fighting for every breath inside. He wrote to Stan Booker, one of our group: "The train stopped at the mouth of a tunnel, a long tunnel, and we were marched through by torchlight and gunpoint. In this tunnel was a train of cattle trucks closely guarded by SS Goons and full of people. It was like a scene from Dante's Inferno."

But Dante's picture of hell had a sign that said "Abandon All Hope," and we suddenly once again had hope. We could breathe, and slowly the thick smoke that coated our lungs was coughed out. A battle against time was going on between the guards and the Resistance fighters who were watching nearby. The Resistance was waiting for help to arrive so they could use their few and precious weapons against the guards who held us. The guards were quickly organizing us into a march that would take us to another train and secure themselves against an attack, one they felt certain would come at any moment.

Their hurry and concern was made clear in the barking orders they gave.

Many men in our car were ordered to pick up the heavy packs of equipment that the Germans were carrying on the train. Those packs contained their weapons, food, ammunition, clothing, and other gear. Packs of 60 pounds or more were placed on the sweaty backs of our men, while other men were pulled aside as hostages.

"We will shoot every one of these men if anyone tries to escape," the guards warned. We knew they were serious. They kept the hostages directly in front of their pointed rifles throughout the march, and no one decided that an escape attempt was worth taking the lives of dozens of fellow prisoners. So we marched into the dark night, along a narrow roadway that went around a steep hill. It was a long march, I couldn't tell at the time, but later found it was about six kilometers or four miles. I was not burdened down with a heavy pack of enemy material, but the march was tiring and the August heat lingered well into the night. Still, it was so wonderful to be out of that tunnel and off that overcrowded train that I hoped we could march all the way into Germany rather than getting on another train.

As we marched, the Resistance fighters watched helplessly from the top of the hill. Tears streamed down their faces as those they had been asked to rescue tramped further and further from freedom. "Wait," they must have begged us under their breaths, "Stall, do anything to slow this down." But we marched on, oblivious to how we were losing our last real chance of rescue to an impending fate worse than anything we could possibly imagine.

In the now dim light of very early morning we could see another train ahead. There were sounds of disappointment and despair as we saw that the train waiting for us was made up of the dreaded 40 by 8 cattle cars. Somehow I had dared to hope that it would be a passenger train or at least a train with boxcars that might be more comfortable and dignified than a cattle train. The packs were taken off the exhausted men who carried them, the hostages returned with relief to their compatriots and once again we were pushed with shouts and harsh orders back into the cars. Once again, we were overcome with the stench of unwashed bodies and the stench of an open bucket toilet. The train jerked forward with moans and scraping metal, and the journey began again.

One of the prisoners had his heart lifted during the march in the dark.

Pierre Lefaucheux, the Paris Resistance leader, discovered that his wife was following the train on her bicycle. The stop in the tunnel allowed her to catch up. In the confusion of getting off the train and marching around the mountain near the Marne river, she found her husband among the prisoners and was able to hug him and give him reassurances of her determination to rescue him. Now, as we once again picked up speed toward Germany, she was back on her bicycle following behind.

Life, such as it was, settled back into a routine of jerky starts, long waits and occasional opportunities to get off the train and perform our natural functions before loading back up again. One car near us had been given a hammer to work on some minor repairs, but they took this opportunity to loosen some floorboards in their car. They returned the hammer knowing that now they could open up the floorboards enough to escape from underneath the train. They decided the safest time to do that with the least chance of detection was while the train was underway. One by one, the men on that train slipped out, sliding onto the ground under the train and letting all the cars following pass over them. Then, they picked themselves up and ran. But at one of the stops, an alert guard noticed that there was some luggage from one of the men far down the track. Each car was immediately searched and the loose floorboard discovered. The guards were beside themselves with anger.

Some of the guards had immediately taken off down the tracks to try and recapture those who had escaped. Six Frenchmen and one American who served in the Royal Canadian Air Force had eased themselves out through the floorboard. We heard rifle shots off in the distance, but as far we knew then and now, the escapees were successful. However, things got very rough for those left in that car. They were pushed to one end of the car while the car was searched and the loose floorboard discovered. They were told they would all be shot. Everything was taken from them — all their clothing, food, water bucket, toilet bucket, everything. The journey continued until the train stopped again and the prisoners from the escapee car, completely naked, were ordered to line up alongside the train. Guards with machine gun rifles stood opposite them, and we all waited for the shooting to begin. The men in that lineup knew that they were facing their last moments on earth. But the order to shoot never came. They were instead ordered to answer nature's call, then were loaded back into the car, still naked as birth, with the order to stay away from the little openings at the ends of the cars.

Those windows offered not only a bit of a view of the passing countryside, but they also offered delicious gulps of fresh air that was somewhat free of the overwhelming odor in the rest of the car. Being able to get close to that window, look out and breathe deeply was a pleasure that we tried to get as often as we could. Jim Hastin was at the window of our car when a shot rang out.

A 17-year-old French boy had put his hand out the window of the car with the loose floorboard. A guard, seeing the hand, had shot it. Screaming in pain and fear, the boy pulled his bloody hand in. The train came to another grinding stop, and a Canadian flyer trained in first aid, Harry Bastable, yelled at the guards for medical help for the young man. Soon the door to the car was unlocked and opened, and the terrified boy was ordered off the train with his hands up, blood streaming down his arm from his wound. Guards surrounded him, asking if he was French or English. He answered, and the officer nodded to the other guards. Two of them pointed at the bushy bank below the tracks, indicating that they wanted him to go down off the tracks. He scrambled down the brush-covered bank. When he got to the bottom, he half-turned as if to ask if this is where they wanted him. The guard motioned him on, and the moment he turned to go on a shot rang out. The first shot hit him in the back and pushed him forward, the second slammed into the back of his head. While quivering on the ground, three more shots were fired into the naked young boy to make certain of the final result. Two of our guys — Leo Grenon and an RAF flyer by the name of Rowe — were ordered out of the car and given spades. While the guards stood by and sickened prisoners such as Jim Hastin watched and told us what was going on, the two dug a shallow grave. The hole was just one spade deep when they were told it was good enough. The young man's body was pushed into it and covered by the gravelly dirt of the railroad bank. Without further ceremony or anything to mark the final resting place of a life cut far too short, the men were loaded back into the car. The train started with another vicious jerk, but this time there was a darkness, sorrow and gritty determination amongst the passengers. This was serious. Life meant nothing to these animals who guarded us. Geneva Convention? We were far from its protection. No one knew where we were, and the further we traveled east into the heart of the country that had darkened the whole world, the more hopeless our situation felt.

The train went on, stopping, starting, waiting. We talked some and slept in brief moments, our legs collapsing, our elbows, shoulders, armpits, hairy bodies, bony knees and sweaty, hairy heads banging into and poking each other. And, always, the continual stench and heat. Still, we had some hope — hope that the train would stop finally and we would be welcomed as fellow prisoners and flyers into a POW camp with a bed, food, some semblance of cleanliness, a little medical care and perhaps even some Red Cross packages. The Red Cross would get word to our families that we were safe and healthy and here for the duration of the war. As the days and nights wore on, that picture became brighter and brighter even as something in the back of my head felt like it might be too good to be true. Could facing a POW camp with such anticipation be a fantasy? What a strange thing, but such as it was on that endless train ride.

We crossed the Rhine at Strasburg and a day or so later traveled through the destroyed city of Frankfurt. The destruction from Allied bombing was almost complete. The center of the city had been laid waste and was just a blackened hole filled with rubble. Bare walls were standing as if they were grave markers, with nothing left for them to hold up.

The next morning the train stopped, and we got word that we had arrived. But where? The women were taken off the train. Many husbands and wives that were part of the Resistance, or thought to be, were arrested together and now they were allowed to find each other and say goodbye. The women were to be taken on a different train to Berlin, the men were to stay with this train. The heart-rending goodbyes were permanent for most of them.

We were moved onto several different tracks before the train started again and soon entered forested land. We passed some men working on the line wearing strange clothing, shirts and trousers with large blue and white stripes. Prisoners.

It was late afternoon, another sweltering mid-August day, when the train stopped once more, now for the last time. We were ordered out and lined up once more for the count. We could tell that this was not just another stop on the way. The activity surrounding — all the guards, the men working in those filthy striped uniforms, the high fences with barbed wire, the dingy gray factory buildings — all told us that this is where we had been headed all along. If this was a POW camp, I had been fooling myself. As I stood in line, looking around, another pit of fear and doubt filled my very empty stomach.

07 FARM BOY TO FIGHTER

Someone standing on the platform at the train station in Buchenwald, someone from today's time and world and not that time and world, would have observed the disturbing sight of 2000 human beings who somewhere along the way of that five-day journey had begun to lose their humanity. Without dignity, one quickly loses the sense of being a member of the human race. It takes far less than most imagine to lose the sense of superiority we typically experience of being far above the beasts of the field and the air. We are not bugs, not birds or dogs or cattle, and this seems instinctively clear to us until we are treated as such. Our sense of ourselves depends remarkably on how those around us view us.

We emerged from that train stiff and sore from lack of exercise and from traveling crumpled together like so much garbage. Most of us, myself included, were suffering from diarrhea, and we all bore evidence on our bodies not only of our own sickness, but that of our fellow passengers. There was hardly an item of clothing that if seen today would not be instantly thrown into a landfill. We were wildly hungry and thirsty and completely and utterly exhausted. Cattle emerging from a long journey in such overcrowded and filthy conditions would hardly have looked, smelled or acted much different than we did when we clambered off the cars onto the tracks of the train station at Buchenwald.

It was the end of our journey, and while the initial impressions were anything but encouraging, at that point we could not imagine that anything could possibly be worse than continuing on that train. So we emerged, tentatively moving legs and arms, trying to work out the soreness that had accumulated over the past days, while following the barking orders to lineup. Once again, we were counted. I was a number, and I felt like a number, a German number, that is all. I was empty of any value to the man facing me other than to verify that the SS guards had done their job of delivering the load from Paris to this place.

But who was I really? And how did I find myself, a 22-year-old farm boy from Ferndale, Washington, here at this horrible spot on the planet in the complete control of these people who valued my life less than the flies in the air. Like most of us on that train and standing here now being counted, I had contemplated that question during the many uncomfortable hours of that agonizing journey.

My dad, Joseph Melchior Moser, came to Washington State from Switzerland in 1911 when he was about 27 years old. The Mosers are a good Swiss Catholic family, and my father left an extended family in the town of Sattel, an area about 50 miles east of Zurich.

He came first to Kent, Washington, just south of Seattle, where he worked as a farm hand on a dairy farm. He had come to America because there were too many children in the Moser family back in Sattel to inherit the farm. There were more opportunities to create a life in the US, and he was drawn to the small Swiss immigrant communities scattered around the Seattle area. Besides people who shared his culture and background, the geography with the nearby snowcapped mountains, fields filled with dairy cattle and mild if wet climate, appealed to the young Swiss farmer. One of the families from the same region in Switzerland as the Mosers was the Imhof family. After immigrating first to New Zealand, Frank Imhof took his family to Ferndale, Washington, just eight miles south of the Canadian border and practically right on the cold, clear waters of Northern Puget Sound.

The Imhof family had a big farmhouse, and when the double doors from the parlor and the living room were opened up, the large room served as an excellent dance floor. The Swiss Catholics loved to dance. One day Joe Moser traveled about 90 miles north to participate in the dance at the Imhof farm.

My dad was 38 then. A small and lean man with dark hair and a dark moustache who smoked a pipe incessantly, wearing down the tooth he used to clamp down on the pipe, and was fond of homemade whisky. He also loved to dance. On that night he danced with a lively young lady named Mary Imhof. Young is right, because she was just 15 and, at age 38, Joe was into his middle years as measured then. But things happened fast to the unlikely couple, and in June of 1921 they were married.

On September 13, 1921, Joe and Mary welcomed their first-born son into the world, and in good Swiss tradition named him after Joe's father: Joseph Frank Moser. That's me. I've always explained that the reason I am so short is that my mom had only a three-month pregnancy. While such events were no doubt scandalous in the small, religious community — and especially so because of the age difference — such happenings were more frequent than most adults of that time talked openly about.

Dad had moved up to Ferndale after meeting my mother and started farming on his own, renting a farm on the Lummi Indian Reservation known as the 101 Ranch. After I was born, my grandfather, Frank Imhof, decided to move to a new home about a mile from where he was farming, and so Dad and Mom took over his farm and we moved into my grandparents' house. With his first son, dad had some help for the growing farm work, and I can tell you that I started very early. I was joined by sister Louise in 1924, then sister Josephine in 1927, brother Frank in 1931 and sister Rosalee in 1935. Tragedy struck early and hard in our family. At just 15 months of age, darling little sister Josephine carried some apples to the water trough used to feed the horses. Without anyone noticing, she climbed up into the trough and drowned. It is hard to say what affect this kind of grief has on a family, on relationships between husband and wife and on the outlook of children who at the age we were saw only wonder and delight in the world we were discovering. But it cast a pall over what was otherwise an almost idyllic farm life in one of the most beautiful places in the world.

Dad died in the summer of 1936 when he was just 53. I was about to be a sophomore in high school, but I was already heavily involved in the dairy farming operation. By now we were milking 45 cows and had some of the most advanced farming technology in the region. We already had the latest and greatest milking machines, powered by a generator. The year before my dad died, we installed electricity to run the machines and light the barn. The machines made the workload easier, but not much because we were always adding more calves, chickens, pigs, horses, geese and other animals to the farm. My dad was definitely of the old school. In addition to being short and very strong, he was exceptionally quiet and a no-nonsense father. We definitely had to tow the mark when dad was around, but he worked hard all the time and was a faithful member of St. Joseph Catholic church in

Ferndale. We noticed he had started to cough, and it got progressively worse until one day, while walking between the house and the barn, the coughing fit turned into throwing up blood. My dad had pneumonia and died a few days later.

I entered Ferndale High School in August of 1935 before I turned 15. I was crazy about sports and was worried that with the pressure on my mom to keep up the farm with a houseful of small kids I would not be able to participate in sports. The burden of all the farm labor had fallen on my mom and myself, with sister Louise in the seventh grade helping out as much as she could. My mom hired a man by the name of Johnny Taylor to help with the milking, and she reduced the herd to 35 cows. This helped with the long hours somewhat but also reduced the income needed to support our family.

I was all of five foot two and 120 pounds that fall of 1936 after my dad died, but I turned out for football. It meant every night after a hard turnout I had to run almost five miles down the country road past my Grandpa Frank Imhof's farm on the Imhof and Slater roads, all the way back to our farm off the Slater Road. Then I had to help with the chores, eat dinner and get up before five a.m. to help with the morning milking before catching the school bus at the end of the one-third mile long driveway. Basketball was out of the question because the games were at night and I had to milk cows, but at 5'2" my basketball career was not likely to soar. I also played baseball all through high school and was pretty good at it, moving up from second base to shortstop in my senior year. Football is a huge thing in our little town of Ferndale; a highlight of community life then as it is now. So playing starting halfback on the Ferndale football team my senior year, at a height of 5'3" and all of 130 pounds, was a really big thing to me. Despite the very busy schedule filled with lots of hard, physical labor, I kept up my grades pretty well and was on the honor roll almost every term through my high school years.

Tragedy was never far away from our household, it seemed. We had lost my sister at just 15 months of age and my dad when I was entering my second year of high school. My uncle Arnold, my mother's brother, died of a tumor in 1937 at the age of about 20. In the summer of 1939, my mother lost two more of her brothers, Ed and Carl. They were killed in a car crash near Lake

Samish coming back from a Swiss wrestling match in Portland. It was late at night coming back and a long drive from Portland, but they couldn't get anyone to milk the cows for them so they pushed on despite being drowsy. I was supposed to go with them but couldn't get away from all the work because by this time we had lost our hired man and my mom and I had to do all the farm work ourselves. Although they were my uncles, Ed and Carl were more like cousins or brothers as they were only three and four years older than me. The week before I had gone with them to Tacoma to the match but couldn't leave my mom with all the chores two weekends in a row.

Their older brother, Joe, was driving and fell asleep about 10 miles from home. The car plowed into the back of a flatbed truck, and Ed and Carl were killed. Then Grandpa Frank, Mom's father, died in 1940. Sometimes, particularly when thinking of my mom back home and the telegrams she must be getting after I was shot down, I wondered how such a little lady could be so strong. How much grief can one woman bear? Yet she did bear it, and with grace and strength. I saw her pray the Rosary and faithfully attend Mass, and I knew that her trust in God was crucial to her dealing with the heavy burdens placed on her. Watching my mother model this kind of faith, steadiness and strength was instrumental in dealing with my own torment while in German hands.

When 1939 turned to 1940, I was a senior in high school. I had been elected Student Body Treasurer, was a two-year starter on the football team, the starting shortstop on the baseball team and life was pretty good. Despite the hard work and sorrows that hung over our farm like late fall mist, I was optimistic about life and eager to see what I might accomplish. I loved airplanes and subscribed to an airplane magazine. About this time I saw a picture of a new experimental fighter plane that the Army Air Corps was investigating. It had two engines, twin booms that swept back to a rounded tail. A canopy streamed sleekly above a smooth metal fuselage. Somehow it conveyed both beauty and menace, and I was hooked. Some may find this hard to believe, but my interest in girls at that time was quite limited. But airplanes, that was another matter. I fell head over heels in love with the Lockheed P-38 and couldn't stop thinking about it. I knew I had to fly that plane.

My love affair with the airplane grew until I found out that you had to have two years of college education in order to qualify for the U.S. Army Air

Corps fighter pilot training. With the farm left to Mom and me — with some help from sister Louise — I had no opportunity to go to college. So I graduated and tried not to let my dreams of the wild blue yonder interfere. My life direction seemed all too inevitable: farm work and more farm work. Not that I hated it — I enjoyed the early mornings, the physical work and especially the more mechanical aspects of farming, particularly now that we had a tractor and had mostly retired the work horses.

Those thoughts changed on December 7, 1941. When the Japanese launched the sneak attack on Pearl Harbor, they thrust the U.S. into the war in Europe as well as the Pacific. Suddenly, Uncle Sam wanted fighter pilots and dropped the college requirements for pilot training. Instead, they offered a test, which if passed with an 82% grade, allowed you to enter pilot training, assuming you could pass the physical. By that time, Mom had also decided the farm was too much for her. Perhaps she was also concerned about how she would manage if I had to go to war. The farm was sold, and mom had taken a job. So I was free from that obligation and traveled to Seattle to take the pilot examination.

I was heartsick when informed that I had only scored 74%. How could it be? My dreams at night had been filled with diving my P-38 into gaggles of Messerschmitts and Focke-Wulfes, and now those dreams were dashed. Now the fact that we were no longer farming meant I didn't have a job at home that would keep me out of the Army, so I waited unhappily for the draft notice. I started checking into the Navy, hoping that while I probably couldn't fly my favorite airplane with the Navy, I might at least still be a fighter pilot. The draft notice finally came and with heavy heart I felt my fate as a foot soldier was sealed. But the same day my draft notice arrived, I received a letter from the Army Air Corp recruiting office in Seattle informing me that they had made an error in grading my examination. I had actually gotten an 84% grade, and they wanted to know if I was still interested in Army Air pilot training. I couldn't believe it. I went from imagining myself slogging through the mud carrying a rifle through Europe or the Pacific islands to once again dreaming of getting into a P-38. On May 18, 1942, I went to Seattle, passed the physical and was sworn into the Army Air Corp on the same day.

It would be 21 months of intensive training before I was a full-fledged fighter pilot assigned to my dream plane, the P-38. First, there were 11 weeks of intensive physical training and schooling in Santa Ana, California. Then, for primary flight training I was sent to Sequoia Field in Visalia, California. I didn't know it until years later, but the Commandant of Cadets at Visalia Field while I was a cadet was a Lt. Ward L. Vander Griend, the head of a prominent family in Lynden, Washington, which is right next to Ferndale. We started our flight training in a Ryan PT-22, an open-cockpit tail-dragger. After about 10 hours of instruction, we were expected to be able to fly solo, and I reached my 10 hours without soloing. My instructor, Mr. Bodily, told me that he was going to have to wash me out. I was simply flying too mechanically and didn't seem to be getting the natural feel of the airplane that was needed to become an instinctive fighter pilot. I wrote my Mom that night, with sickening disappointment, that I was washed up as a pilot.

The next morning Mr. Bodily told me we were going up for one last try. But instead of taking off together, at the end of the taxiway he stopped me and got out. It was time to find out if I could fly this airplane alone. I took off with my heart pounding wildly. The first time you are up in the air looking back at the ground and realizing that your only hope of getting back down safely is by relying on your own skills is an amazingly frightening feeling. You either get a grip on your fears and focus on the job at hand, or you let fear take over with disastrous results. By the time I put that airplane down, I think I could have flown without wings I was so excited. I took her around again now thinking I had this flying thing licked. Too mechanical? Hah, I'll show them what flying is all about, I thought. But, I was too inexperienced to pay attention to the crosswind blowing across the runway, and when I touched down for the second time, the wind caught my wing and spun the low wing trainer around like a top. Somehow, the wings didn't touch the ground or it would have been ugly, but this maneuver, called a ground loop, landed me my cadet nickname, which stuck with me through the rest of training. Now I was known as "Ground Loop Joe." It was a humbling reminder never to think that I have things all figured out.

The open cockpit of the P-22 provided an interesting highlight of my training days. One of my buddies had soloed his plane the day before, so he and his instructor went up to start working on aerobatic maneuvers. When they reached altitude, the instructor told Jack to do a roll, which he did. He heard nothing from the instructor in the back seat, so he did another. Still no comment, so he did it once more. Finally he turned around to find out why the instructor was so silent. The back seat was empty. The instructor had neglected to fasten his shoulder harness and had fallen out when the plane went inverted. Fortunately, parachutes were part of our equipment so it all ended well for the very embarrassed instructor.

After two and a half months, we were sent on to Minter Field in Bakersfield, California for more advanced training. It was brutally hot in Bakersfield with temperatures topping 100 degrees daily. But the trainer we were flying now, the BT-13 Vultee Valiant, nicknamed the Vibrator for obvious reasons, was a big step up in horsepower and navigation equipment. Fortunately for forgetful instructors, it even had an enclosed canopy. Two months later we were sent to Chandler Field, near Phoenix for more advanced training in an AT-6 and an AT-9. These were bigger, more powerful planes, and the AT-9 was equipped with instruments for flying at night or in the clouds; this training would come in very handy while flying in the clouds and fog of England and Europe. Finally we transitioned to early versions of the P-38 in our final phase of flight training. We were now into gunnery practice, and the reality of flying a powerful fighting machine with real firepower was dawning on me.

On October 1, 1943, I and my 47 fellow classmates of 43-I became commissioned officers in the Army Air Corps — 2nd Lieutenants. We received our wings and were officially designated as fighter pilots for the United States of America. After 10 days' leave to Los Angeles, highlighted by lost luggage that was never found, I was assigned to Van Nuys field just over the Hollywood Hills from Hollywood. On October 14, we were assigned to the 474th Fighter Group, forming the 428th, 429th and 430th Fighter Squadrons. I was in the 429th. Our assigned aircraft, of course, was the P-38. Finally, the dream of my high school years, which now seemed so far in the distant past, had been realized. I felt fulfilled, that this was right, that my life was on track and I was in the place that destiny had meant for me. Captain Burl Glass was my squadron commander, and Captain Merle Larson, a veteran of the air war over North Africa was my flight leader. I had all these guys up on a pedestal, but no one more than Captain Larson — he was an outstanding pilot, and I knew from his exploits in North Africa that he was a great fighter, brave and resourceful. It would be easy following him into combat.

Van Nuys airfield was a converted orchard, and while the fall weather was beautiful, the training was intense. We knew it was only a matter of time until it would be for real, that we would climb into our cockpits, fire up the powerful twin engines and face the threat of skilled and experienced enemy fighters eager to end our brief careers. The seriousness of the business we were in was brought home with the deaths of two of my roommates from training accidents. We were young, hotshot pilots, and the reason they send 20-year-old kids to war is because with youth comes a sense of invulnerability. But these deaths were like losing brothers. We were in training with these guys for almost two years, and we became a very close-knit group. We knew them better than our own family in many ways. We knew their hopes and fears, knew what made them tick. And now they were gone. With these deaths we also had a feeling that this sorrow we were experiencing would not be our last.

On January 1, 1944, I took advantage of the fact that I was only a few miles away from Pasadena to go to the Rose Bowl. I was glad I went, even though USC trounced our University of Washington Huskies by a score of 29-0. But I was glad because it kept me out of some trouble. One of the pilots of our group decided that the Rose Bowl would be a good event for some practice bombing and dropped a small practice bomb onto the field. Ten of our pilots were in the air that day, and they came under some very serious questioning. Since I was at the game, I was cleared, but the guilty pilot never was identified, so the consequences fell on the whole unit. We were young, and in some cases, stupid. Incidences like this demonstrated in whose hands the fate of freedom rested.

After the ground loop the day of my solo flight, my training went pretty much without incident. Well, there was that time I made the foolish mistake of eating a big meal of wieners and sauerkraut for lunch before going up on a training flight. By this time we had been assigned to Lomita Field near Long Beach, and three of us were assigned to fly to Palmdale in the desert near Edwards Air Base. I was Flight Leader, which meant the two with me would follow every step of the way as we flew in formation. We were at about 18,000 feet flying over the San Bernardino mountains when the altitude and the sauerkraut combined in an unpleasant way. Despite being a big fighter, the P-38 cockpit is pretty cramped and the only place I had to deposit that unfortunate lunch was between my knees. I ripped off my oxygen mask and microphone, pushed the control stick forward to make room for my head between my knees. The plane, of course, went into a dive, which I couldn't help under the circumstances. But as the flight leader my two wingmen dutifully followed my plane into a dive. When I could lift up my head, I saw that we were heading toward the mountains coming up at us fast and I pulled up with my wingmen following. They were on the radio yelling at me, "Joe, what's going on?" Before I could get my mask and microphone back on, another wave of sauerkraut hit, and the dive began again. We went into five dives before my lunch was completely deposited on the cockpit floor. All the while my wingmen were on the radio frantically asking me what the heck was going on and dutifully following my every gyration. When I told them, they were relieved and laughing like crazy.

However, flying with that kind of mess is hardly a laughing matter. When we landed in Palmdale, two ground crew sergeants came up and asked if there was anything they could do for me.

"Sure," I said. "You can clean up this mess."

One of them stuck his head in the cockpit to see what mess I was referring to and almost fell off the plane. They rather impolitely refused. So, I had to clean it myself, cursing my menu choice all the while.

Flying out of Palmdale was now part of our training regime, and we were assigned to help test the radar that was installed at Edwards. This was a relatively new invention, and it was installed to help detect the arrival of enemy aircraft from the West — Japanese, of course. We were given the role of defenders of the sprawling air base, and the Marine fighters were the designated attackers. They would come in over the Pacific, the radar was supposed to pick them up and then we were scrambled to intercept them. The second day of these games I was determined to be the first in the air once the alarm sounded. So in my hurry I neglected one important part of the normal take-off routine. At the end of the taxiway and before rolling onto the active runway, we stopped, revved the engines and cleared the sparkplugs of carbon buildup. I taxied out fast, continued rolling and pushed those twin throttles forward. Instead of being airborne halfway down the runway as would have been normal, the plane just didn't seem to want to get in the air. The end of the runway was coming up and I still wasn't up to flying speed. I watched it get closer and closer and finally decided that this bird just wasn't going to fly that day, so I cut the throttles and jumped on the brakes. But I hit the end of the runway at 80 or 90 miles an hour. I bounced through a field, plowed through a fence, went across a highway, jumped a ditch and came to rest in a field. I wanted out of that plane badly, as I was afraid of fire, but my legs were shaking so badly that it took 10 minutes for them to settle down enough to allow me the strength to crawl out of the plane. I still wonder why I wasn't reprimanded or worse for that; I guess Uncle Sam needed pilots, and they had a real investment in me by that time.

You would have thought that scare would have taken some of the piss and vinegar out of a young hotshot fighter pilot, but it was only a week or so later when I made an even worse mistake that nearly cost me my life. The P-38 was a fabulous flying machine, in fact, it was the airplane that Richard Bong used in the Pacific war to become the US's all time leading fighter ace with 40 kills. But many pilots complained about it. The cockpit was unheated, and it was dreadfully cold to fly, particularly at high altitudes and in the European theater with the cold winters. But a more serious problem, particularly with the earlier models, was something called compressibility. This was a flight characteristic that made it almost impossible to pull out of a steep dive at high speeds. The controls became frozen so that even the strongest pilot couldn't get enough leverage to pull the plane out of the dive. The speed build-up would cause the tail to come apart and the plane would be lost — too often with the pilot. It cost a number of deaths in combat and training before the design flaw was finally fixed with dive flaps installed on planes in the field, and finally in production models shortly before the end of the war.

I discovered this problem for myself during one memorable training mission. I was flying alone and wanted to find out just how high this plane would go, so I took it all the way up to 31,600 feet. Today, with airliner travel routinely done at that altitude and higher, it doesn't seem like such a big deal. But in those days, with a freezing, unpressurized cockpit, leather flying gear and oxygen mask providing the needed oxygen above 10,000 feet, that was really up there. I tried, but I couldn't coax the craft any higher. I flew at this altitude for awhile, enjoying the astounding view, when I foolishly decided I would also try and find out today just how fast this thing could come down. We had been warned somewhat about the compressibility problem and were advised against pushing the plane's speed envelope. We were told if the plane started to vibrate violently, it was only a matter of seconds before she would break up in flight. Heedless, I tipped her down into a dive.

The empty weight of the 38 was almost 13,000 pounds, and maximum takeoff weight is over 20,000 pounds. She is pushed by two 1475 horsepower V-12 engines, so it didn't take long for the speed to build up. The spec sheet says maximum speed is 414 miles per hour, the fastest fighter in the European theater until the Germans introduced the Me-262, the first jet fighter late in the war. When my bird hit about 575 miles per hour, she started to shake like crazy and I knew I had pushed her too far. Now remembering the warnings of training, I started sweating like crazy and pulled the throttles all the way back and hauled back on the stick with all my strength to try and slow the dive. But my sweat and the high altitude caused the windshield and the side glass of the canopy to frost over, and I was suddenly flying blind. Even though ground temperature in California at that time was about 70 degrees, at 30,000 feet it was 20 to 25 degrees below zero. I continued to haul back on the stick, not knowing what my flying attitude was, if I was still diving, climbing, rolling, upside down or what. The plane finally stopped shaking, so I knew I was not in immediate danger of the plane falling apart, but those mountains were high and I had no idea where they were. When I got down to almost 10,000 feet, the glass started to clear off just a bit and I could see I was still in a shallow dive. I was very grateful to get back to Palmdale that day, and while I never told my fellow pilots what happened, I did advise them to avoid steep dives.

The blissful, if sometimes frightening days of California training were finally concluded in February, 1944. We knew our time would come to be shipped to the front, and that day came on February 15. We left California for Boston by train — a train ride that seemed anything but luxurious at the time, but in retrospect was a comfortable, carefree journey compared to the one that had just ended for those of us on that prison train from Fresnes.

The barking dogs, straining at the leashes of their handlers, lined both sides of the roadway that we marched down after we stiffly unloaded from the cattle train. They snarled at us viciously, and the guards enjoyed our discomfort at their proximity. Beyond the dogs was a barbed wire fence and beyond that an endless row of dingy, grayish-brown wood factory buildings. But along the fence I could also see the faces of those on the other side, and what I saw shocked me and chilled me to my soul. They did not look like POWs, indeed, with their skulls practically showing through their paper-thin skin, the dim, empty eyes, their meaningless stares, I hardly felt they were human. I was a cow coming off a dirty train, but these were ferrets, captured and awaiting a deadly fate. A Ferndale farm boy and hotshot fighter pilot no longer — like the pitiful creatures behind that fence, I was just trash to be disposed of in the German system of waste management.

08 BUCHENWALD

The dogs were the first thing I saw after getting off that train. Big German shepherds restrained by strong collars and leashes held by SS guards. If the guards could have snarled with the frothy, spit-filled, teeth-bared growl of the dogs, I'm sure they would have. There were two rows of dogs and guards with just enough room between them for us to walk without getting torn apart. This was the gauntlet we walked through when we arrived in Buchenwald.

We, of course, thought we were going to a Prisoner of War camp; that our life would be quiet and simple, with respectful wardens and continual whispered plotting of how we would escape and rejoin the fight. And we would be fed three decent meals a day, which right now was one of my greatest concerns. We knew nothing of concentration camps or death camps and certainly had no reason to believe any such thing would be our destiny. The world knew little to nothing of such atrocities on August 20, 1944, when we arrived. It would not know of such places and the Nazi plan to exterminate the world's Jews and all others it hated until almost eight months after I arrived, on April 11, 1945. That's when the first of these camps was liberated — Buchenwald. Because it was the first to be liberated, the camp was visited during the first three weeks after the liberation by reporters, photographers, officers, U.S. Congressional delegations, British Parliamentary delegations and many others. This was because General Eisenhower, after touring the camp on April 13, just two days after its liberation, determined that it was necessary that the world see the unbelievable atrocities of Hitler's regime. He and others who first visited the camp were concerned that no one would believe them if they simply described what they saw. More eyes had to be there, more noses to smell it, if the world was to take this horror seriously.

Eisenhower was so disturbed by what he saw that it was the main topic of conversation with Winston Churchill when the two met a few days after

Eisenhower visited the camp, which was still filled with prisoners. They decided to rush a group of British journalists and members of Parliament to Buchenwald to see that the horrors there were greater than anyone could describe. And so Buchenwald became famous the world over, a symbol of the darkness the human soul is capable of.

Buchenwald was not a death camp like Auschwitz, Treblinka, Belzec, and others. The death camps were much smaller than concentration or labor camps because they never were intended to house people for labor. They had a single purpose: kill and dispose of as many people — mostly Jews — as the technology of the time permitted. Buchenwald, like Dachau and Bergen-Belsen, was a camp originally intended to house political prisoners. It contained large industrial factories as part of or adjacent to the camp to take advantage of the "free" labor offered by the prisoners. Dachau was the first of these created by the Nazi party in March, 1933. Buchenwald was created in 1937 with German communists, the hated political opponents of Nazism, as its primary intended victims. Though created as a political prison and a work camp, Buchenwald in practice crossed the line between a work prison and extermination camp. An estimated 56,000 prisoners died in the camp among the approximately 250,000 who were imprisoned. And a special method for efficient killing of Russian prisoners of war was devised. Most prisoners died, however, due to the horribly unsanitary conditions and brutal work without much in the way of food or medical care. In other words, they were both worked and starved to death.

I knew none of this walking through the line of vicious guards and their more vicious dogs. I just knew we were off the train, and for that I was grateful. But as we were marched toward the main camp I could see beyond the line of dogs and guards an imposing fence and the dull gray-brown weathered wood of factory buildings. Now we see only black and white images from these places, but there was a dull grayness, a dinginess, and heaviness to the buildings that filled me with a sense of foreboding, despite my almost joyful relief at getting off that train. There was a heavy dread deep in my gut when I looked beyond the guards and through the fence at the faces staring at us: hundreds and hundreds of empty, vacant, bony skeleton faces. No smiles of encouragement. No empathy or pity.

Nothing recognizably human in those faces. Just empty, dead stares. For a moment I wondered, could this happen to me? Could I be reduced to such a state? If this was a POW camp, it was far, far worse than anything I imagined when trying to prepare myself to be a prisoner.

We did not enter the main gate of Buchenwald, the gate made famous in many pictures and captured in many tourist's photo albums since then, including mine. In the stucco above the heavy iron gates were the words: "Recht oder Unrecht mein Vaderland." It means, "Right or wrong, this is my country." The iron gate itself contained the wrought iron inscription: "Jedem Das Seine," translated literally as "To each his own," or "To each his due." It is not as famous as the slogan over the gate to Auschwitz: "Arbeit Macht Frie" or "Work Makes One Free." But its cryptic message leaves much room for interpretation. The inscription's origin is from ancient Rome, but what made them embed these words in the gate through which nearly a quarter million prisoners would enter? To each his own? Was it a statement of simple fate, that whatever happens to someone is just what it is? No meaning, no purpose, no real lasting value? Does it mean that those who end up in this hell on earth somehow have deserved it? That, somehow, in some twisted mind this camp represented justice? It is still inconceivable, almost 64 years after arriving at that place, to think that any human heart could become so hardened and hate-filled to think that a fellow human being could ever deserve such treatment.

We did not see that sign when we entered Buchenwald from the train station because we entered by the gate just past the camp zoo and just to the east of the crematorium. I didn't know as I walked by this building that it was a crematorium — the final stop for most of the more than 50,000 human beings whose lives ended here in what should be a peaceful tract of forest outside the medieval city of Weimar. I did see a chimney with thick smoke coming out of it. And I did smell something nauseatingly sweet and burnt. Of course I did not identify it as the smell of human flesh burning, but it was a smell that completely dominated the entire camp. I could not believe, as strong as it was, that the residents of Weimar, some six miles to the southeast, could not smell it when the wind was blowing that direction. That smell has stayed with me all my life, leading to a lifelong hatred of the smell of fried bacon.

One of the guards who spoke English told one of us flyers as we marched by that building with the smoking chimney that we would never leave this place except as smoke from that chimney. That was how I learned it was a crematorium. It was how I first started to realize that this was probably not a prisoner of war camp but something far worse than anything we could have imagined. It was a place where men and children were starved, worked to death and executed. Somehow, for reasons we could not understand, we had found ourselves in the deepest, darkest part of the heart of Nazi evil and hatred. For the next two months I lived with the gnawing reality of that cold statement. It can still chill me these many years later. There were many days, despite my "cup is half full" outlook on life, that I fully believed what that cold-hearted German said.

It was late afternoon when we arrived in Buchenwald. We were marched past the crematorium, past a number of other wood-sided, dirty and drab buildings, until we entered a larger one. This was, as we would soon discover, the disinfection facility. When we entered we were ordered to strip off all our clothes. As I removed my shoe, I saw again the missing toe and wondered if I would see that shoe again, the reminder of my very narrow scrape with death while parachuting from my plane. How long ago that seemed now, another lifetime ago. My clothes were filthy and smelly from my attempt to escape and then five days of far too close contact on the train. I thought a shower and a change of clothes would be good. But I had seen that all the inmates in this asylum wore ill-fitting pajama-like clothes that showed large gray stripes even through the unwashed grime. I'd rather have the smelliest U.S. military uniform possible than such a degrading uniform.

After our clothes were removed we stood in a line, naked as the day of birth. Soon I saw what the line was for: a haircut. It will forever remain the rudest, nastiest, roughest haircut of my life. The "barber" moved quickly from one prisoner to the next without the slightest thought of even wiping off the clogged blades of his heavy, black electric clippers. I soon found myself facing him. Like the inmates, his face too was blank and unsympathetic. The clipper tore into my hair and I grimaced as it scraped and ripped. In a moment my head was bare and soon after so was the growth of beard that grew since I left the airfield a week before.

The uniformed "barber" grunted at me and poked my arm. I raised both arms up and the hair under my arms was similarly half ripped and half cut away. I had seen the treatment of the men before so I knew my groin would receive the same painful treatment, which it did. Every part of me felt raw, scraped extra space, violated and abused. From here we stepped into the showers.

It was a fast and freezing cold shower. There was no soap. We were in a long room and nearly all of us flyers were together. For just a moment, being together and feeling the week of sweat, grime and fear wash off me felt amazingly good. I felt a little life in me yet. And just a bit of hope.

A few minutes later we were in another line. From the stifled groans and cries from the men ahead of me in line, I knew whatever was up was not going to be pleasant. The closer I got the more afraid I became of the procedure that was being performed on my fellow flyers. And then I faced the guard. He was sitting on a stool with a big tub between his knees. He held in his hand a rough brush. I was told to close my eyes. The big brush was dipped into the tub containing a disinfectant, probably lye, and then swabbed over my raw and bloodied body from head to toe. My underarms and crotch burned like I had been stuck with 1000 burning cigarettes or stung by 100 angry bees. Try as I might to keep it inside, I too yelped out in excruciating pain.

Still groaning, naked and terrorized, we were marched to a different building. There they handed us our prisoner uniforms. There was no concern for sizing, and all were dingy gray with those distinctive broad darker gray stripes. They came in two parts, a pants and shirt. Some of the uniforms were large and some were small, and as some of the men were large and some small that would have worked fine if they had made any attempt to match the clothes with the wearer. But size didn't matter to the efficient workers handing out the uniforms. So some big men got a very small pants and large shirt and some who were short got monstrously large pants or shirts. I was given normal-sized pants but a shirt obviously intended for a prisoner much larger than my five foot six frame. It came down nearly to my knees and all that extra fabric was one of the absolute best things that happened to me in Buchenwald, which I will explain later.

Some were given a pair of rough clogs, but most of us got nothing for our feet. Then we were handed a tin bowl about the size of a cereal bowl and told to keep it. All our so-called "meals" were served in this bowl. We were marched past what seemed an endless row of single-story, long, desperately ugly barracks. Along our right side we could see the sentry line and the electric barbed-wire fence. The fence circled around the prisoner section of Buchenwald, an area almost 100 acres in size. In total there were over 60 barracks.

We were marched to an open area at the northeast corner of Little Camp. Little Camp was a section of the barracks where the prisoners received the least food and harshest treatment. As we stood there in the darkening skies of that August evening we waited, expecting to be directed to one of the barracks near this open area. Instead, we were handed a blanket. Or I should say, a third of a blanket because it was made clear that we were to share one blanket between three of us. We looked at each other, puzzled. We're supposed to sleep here? Someone in our group must have been given some instruction as he sat down, and soon we all started to sit down. The ground was not soft, clean dirt, but rocky with larger flat rocks interspersed with gravel. OK, I thought. We'll wait here for a bit until they find some barracks for us. It was not to be. This was our barracks.

One hundred and sixty-eight of us flyers slowly tried to make ourselves comfortable on the rough, rocky ground. Although we carried our tin bowls with us, it was clear we had missed the evening "meal," and so our ever present hunger increased even more. My eyes wandered around looking for an escape route, and I saw others doing the same. Rows and rows of barracks to the south and west. Just beyond us was the Gardening Detail, a place where prisoners worked raising food, not for the inmates but for the SS. Beyond the garden area, about 50 to 75 yards from where we laid, was the 10-foot-high barbed-wire fence that also carried a severe shock. A watchtower was placed every 50 yards along the entire fence perimeter, which itself was over two miles long circling the prisoner area of the camp. SS guards kept a watchful eye from each of these watchtowers. Making any sort of run for it did not look like a smart idea. We would have to wait and see what tomorrow would bring.

I settled in near Jim Hastin. We talked a little about food — always about food — about Jim's vicious bug bites that covered his legs after his lengthy stay in Fresnes prison, about home and family. At least we could be together. It was comforting to share thoughts of home and family with someone who came from the same area and who longed to see his family again as much as I did mine. The August nights were hot and humid, but the heat dissipated after the sun went down and we began to feel the cool dampness of the surrounding forest. We tried to make the one blanket work for three but it was largely hopeless. It could neither protect us against the sharp rocks we were laying on, nor serve as enough of a pillow, or cover us sufficiently to ward off the chill. We drifted off into an uneasy, rock-disturbed sleep — our first night in Buchenwald.

There are some nightmares you wake from that stay with you for hours, even the whole day. This was one nightmare that was to last for two months. I was desperately tired, having gotten no real normal sleep since bailing out of my plane. We woke with the hazy late-August sun coming up early and warming. For those few brief seconds of mental activity between being lost in sleep and growing increasingly conscious of the life you are in, my mind thought, as I'm sure the others did, that this was all a very bad dream. You go from being certain that it is just a dream, to being afraid the nightmare might be real, to the sickening dread of increasing realization that yes, this is indeed my life. There is no escape from it — nor from this place. One by one, we woke up. Now what? A gray, striped mass lying on open, rocky ground surrounded by ugly buildings and an even uglier barbed wire fence. A confused, angry, fearful and terribly hungry gray mass.

We did not have long to wait. Soon kapos came and ordered us to the square where all the inmates are counted. Kapos were prisoners who were "trusties," doing many of the tasks of the guards for special privileges. Many of them were far more cruel and inhumane than the guards themselves. We soon learned the German word "appell," which means roll call. This was the primary method the prisoner officers used to make certain that all the prisoners were accounted for. "Appell" was held in Appell Platz or Roll Call Square, where we would gather twice a day and sometimes more often.

But this interminable time of trying to stand quietly in one place was also used to communicate important messages. Which is why the prisoners lined up for appell faced the whipping block. This was used to punish prisoners and in so doing serve an object lesson for the rest of us. While the whipping block was always there, on "special occasions" a gallows would be rolled into the square so that the inmates could learn a lesson from this method of punishing inmates. Roll Call Square was near the main gate of the camp, at the south end of the prisoners' camp area enclosed by barbed wire. It was a large area, almost four acres. Twice a day, morning and evening, those four acres were filled with the sick, dying, diseased, starving bits of wretched humanity. We faced south, and on our right, just past the machine shop, stood the crematorium with its dirty, thick, acrid smoke pouring out continuously. As bits of heavier ash floated down on us, so did our hopes for a life beyond this misery.

Appell could last anywhere from an hour and a half to five hours, depending on whether or not the guards had everything under control. If prisoners were missing, we would have to stand in one place literally for hours while they scoured the camp for those that were missing. The prisoners went in order of blocks or barracks, but since we did not have a barrack, we hung together as a group.

It was some time after our first morning appell, around noon, that we found out what the "dining service" was like in Buchenwald. A kapo lined us up near a barracks adjacent to our new "home," the patch of rocky soil where we had slept the night before. Many of the kapos were professional criminals and were among the cruelest, nastiest of the tormenters of Buchenwald. The prison was largely run by the kapos, who for the most part worked hard to keep or elevate their positions by demonstrating to the SS officers just how rough they could be on their fellow prisoners. When we got to the kapos with the food we stuck out our tin bowls and they slopped about a cup of "soup" into it. Then we were handed one slice of black bread about one inch thick.

The soup was usually cabbage soup made from dehydrated cabbage. Once in awhile it would be made from turnips or kohlrabi, but usually cabbage. The first time I looked at it I wondered what kind of soup it was. It looked like there was meat in it, small chunks of white meat that looked a little like worms. They were moving, just like worms. Oh no, they were worms. The top of the soup was covered in worms. But I was starving. I hadn't eaten hardly anything in almost a week. I was shaky all over from hunger and I felt I had to get anything I could find into my stomach to try and survive. So I tried to push the worms away from my finger so I could get at the thin gruel underneath. I closed my eyes and let a little of it into my mouth. It was warm but sour and tasteless — more like dishwater than anything I might describe as recognizable food. Then I felt one of those worms squirming in my mouth and I instinctively spewed it all out. I felt a wave of nausea. But I had to eat. Somehow I had to get this down or I would get weaker and weaker and then, well, I knew what that meant. If I ever forgot, the constant stench reminded me. So I tried again and again, but I began to wretch as I tried to force it down. In disgust I tossed the soup onto the ground. But that was the only time I turned down the German idea of a slave worker's meal. After that first attempt, I learned to force it down, worms and all, and strangely enough, after awhile it began to taste good.

The black bread served by the kapos was hardly bread. In fact, it was about 30 to 40 percent sawdust, almost more wood than bread. It was almost as inedible as the soup. But we knew that the part that wasn't wood was badly needed to keep us alive. It was unbelievably difficult, especially at first, to choke it down, but after awhile we learned better how to deal with it. After we got into our barracks, we discovered the best way to get the nutritional value out of the bread and force it down was to slice it into very thin slices, stick it against the wood stoves used to heat the barracks until the sawdust burned off like charcoal. It was a little like eating a barbeque briquette but we knew it was giving us precious strength. We needed every calorie we could get.

After our first meal, we gathered back together in the open area where we had slept. It was about this time that Colonel Philip Lamason stepped forward. Col. Lamason was the senior officer among the 168 of us, a tall, good looking Squadron Leader from the New Zealand Air Force. I consider it one of the greatest blessings of this challenging time to have Col. Lamason as our commander. His quiet, strong but aggressive leadership was a critical factor not only in holding us together but also in facilitating our eventual release.

"Attention!" he said unexpectedly in his clipped New Zealand accent. We instinctively quickly got up, tried to get ourselves in some semblance of order and stood stiffly waiting.

"Gentlemen, we have ourselves in a very fine fix indeed," he went on. "The goons have completely violated the Geneva Convention and are treating us as common thieves and criminals. However, we are soldiers! From this time on, we will also conduct ourselves as our training has taught us and as our nations would expect from us. We will march as a unit to roll call, and we will follow all reasonable commands as a single unit."

Then he proceeded to organize us first by the country we were from. Over each group he made the senior officer our C.O. or Commanding Officer. For us Americans, that was Captain Merle Larson, and I couldn't have been happier to be serving under this outstanding leader. From this moment on we once again became soldiers, now in a tightly knit group experiencing what very few Allied soldiers would experience. It boosted our morale and gave us hope. We might be in these awful prison uniforms and be in the dirtiest, filthiest, most degrading place on earth, but we were soldiers, American soldiers, the best, proudest fighting force on earth.

Lamason didn't do this just to improve our morale but no doubt because he saw it also as his responsibility to carry on his war duties despite these circumstances. His mind was quickly figuring out ways we could either escape or somehow overcome our captors, and if not overcome them, make things as difficult for them as possible. He also no doubt believed that if the right opportunity presented itself, we would be able to operate much more effectively if military discipline and operations were applied. I can say this with some certainty because the actions he took in the days ahead demonstrated clearly that he was not a leader to sit back and accept the fate that seemed to have been prepared for us. He would fight to the very end, and he would lead us into fighting to the very end if that is the way it was to end.

There was another very important value to this imposition of military discipline. Already, hotheads in our group were agitating. Of course we were all bitterly angry and frustrated. We were all but certain that no one knew our whereabouts. Since it had become clear to us that this was not a Luftwaffe prison camp, we believed correctly that we had fallen out of the system. The Red Cross had no contact with us. The U.S. military did not even know such a place as Buchenwald existed, let alone that Allied soldiers could be sent there. That meant that our families had no idea where we were either. They would get their telegrams about their sons, brothers, fathers being missing in action, and the longer the time went by until they were reported by the Red Cross in a POW camp, the more the family was forced to accept the likelihood of their death. Thinking about how my family was dealing with this circumstance was a big part of my frustration and suffering while in Buchenwald, as it was for most of us. But, acting out on these frustrations with aggressive action and angry words against the kapos who were our most immediate guards and tormentors made no sense. It would just get us all in trouble. So the military discipline that Col. Lamason and then Capt. Larson imposed was a great help to all of us.

The first big test we faced as a military unit under the control of our commanding officers came soon after. Within the first couple of days after arriving at Buchenwald, Col. Lamason was informed by the SS guards that we would begin working in the nearby factories. We had seen the factory buildings when we first arrived at the train station before entering the camp. There was a very large factory to our left, or south, as we marched down the railroad tracks to the gauntlet of dogs and guards, and another smaller factory inside the main fence to our right. The large factory south of the main camp area was the Gustloff Works, built in 1943. It was a German industrial factory built adjacent to the camp in order to take advantage of the slave labor provided by the inmates — though the industrial firm had to pay the SS for the labor of the inmates. The smaller factory inside the main camp, just east of the crematorium, was the German Armament Works. It was built and owned by the SS and built not long after the camp was created to usefully employ the labor of the inmates. Where initially the machine shop in the German Armament Works was used to make a variety of items, including luxury items for the SS officers such as large chandeliers, by the time we were there in the later stages of the war, both factories were busy at work producing war materials. The German Armament Works was manufacturing cartridge cases, antitank shells and parts for Messerschmitt aircraft while the Gustloff Works was producing cannons, rifles, pistols and motor vehicles.

The factories together employed 9000 prisoners. Col. Lamason was informed that we would be instructed to join the work crews. Obviously here was a great dilemma. While the reality of constant torture and execution was not well known to us at this time, we knew that refusing to obey our masters would be to put our lives at risk — as if they weren't at risk enough already. But working on the guns and equipment that would be used to kill our fellow soldiers was equally unacceptable. Col. Lamason, no doubt in consultation with Capt. Larson and the other senior officers, informed the guards that we were soldiers and could not and would not participate in war production. I do not know what reaction this caused among the officers of the camp. We were, after all, only 168 among about 80,000 prisoners at this time. While we were very afraid of what this refusal might mean, we were not aware of any reprisals or punishments because of this principled and courageous stance. What I knew and what was shared by everyone I knew is that I was proud to be an American soldier, and Col. Lamason and Capt. Larson were two great leaders who I would have been glad to follow anywhere they asked.

09 AIR RAID

It was 10 minutes to four in the morning on August 24 when 2nd Lt. Maxwell M. Cain, pilot of the B-17 named "Carrie B II," heard of the bombing mission of the day. While still dark, the morning promised to be another warm, late summer day with light haze. For Lt. Cain and his crew of eight young American flyers, this mission would be their sixth together as a crew and the 132nd mission of the 401st Bomber Group. The 401st was part of the Eighth Air Force commanded by General James H. Doolittle, who won fame and the Congressional Medal of Honor for leading the surprise bombing raid on Tokyo in 1942. Lt. Cain's group was stationed at an airbase near the town of Deenethorpe in England, about 60 air miles northwest of London.

As Lt. Cain sat in that briefing he learned that on that day, August 24, the Eighth Air Force would send up over 1300 bombers to targets all around Germany and occupied Europe. The 401st would contribute 39 planes, or three flights of 12 B-17s each, with three spares. These 39 planes would join the attack on a factory known to be building war materials and equipment; a total of 129 planes or almost 10% of the total Eighth Air Force complement that day would be attacking this strategic target. Reports had it that these factories were building parts for the V-2 rocket, radio equipment and ammunition. There were two factories to attack, both located a little north of the town of Weimar and both believed to be part of a sprawling prison labor camp. Bombing would need to be precise in order to avoid unnecessary casualties among the prisoners in the camp.

It was our fourth morning in Buchenwald. We woke again with the sun just rising and the shouts of the kapos calling us to appell. We had no idea that in England a target had been unknowingly placed on our heads and that suddenly we would be caught up in the vast air war that was going on in the skies all over Europe. Certainly we knew all about the air war, and I had been a very active part of it until just 10 days before. But being under the bombs as they were falling was a far different and more terrifying experience than flying above them as a fighter pilot escorting our big buddies, the bombers. I was about to find out just how terrifying that experience could be.

One by one the crew of Carrie B II climbed aboard their big bomber. The B-17 wasn't called a Flying Fortress for nothing. It sported 11 heavy machine guns. Sgt. R. E. Barron climbed aboard through the small hatch in the bottom of the plane and made his way past the full bomb load into the ball turret. This was the machine gun located on top of the plane just behind the cockpit. The turret would spin around, and he had a 360-degree view to spot trouble coming, as long as it came from above, which it almost always did. He wondered, as did the other crewmen, if this would be a quiet and uneventful flight or if they would face mortal danger. It was a long flight deep into Germany, so it was more likely that there would be trouble — not just from the anti-aircraft guns, but from fighters looking to pick off the wounded, vulnerable and the strays.

A little after eight in the morning, the 39 B-17s of Lt. Cain's group taxied out from their revetments, then with the throaty roar of the four big rotary engines, lumbered into the air, each carrying up to 16,000 pounds of bombs. Although it was the sixth mission for this particular flight crew, this bomber, B-17G serial number 42-97344 had already completed 31 combat missions with only one aborted mission. The plane had been built in Seattle, just 80 miles south of where I grew up, and the 401st Bomber Group had originated at Ephrata Air Base in 1943, in eastern Washington state, only about 150 miles over the Cascade Range from my home in Ferndale.

The sun was beginning to warm the air and the camp in the central German woods, as well as the thousands of prisoners who found themselves caught up in Germany's plan to dominate the world and exercise its hatred freely. By the time Lt. Cain's bomber was flying over the English Channel on its way to Buchenwald, the 9000 or so prisoners assigned to the German Armament Works or the Guftloff Works factories were already at work. Many thousands more were hard at work at the quarry — the most brutal and dangerous of all work sites, or at other work sites around the camp including gathering up those who had died during the night and delivering them on carts to join the stack by the crematorium.

For us it seemed to be the start of another day of idleness, limited exercise and lots of talk about home, food, what would happen to us, food, thoughts of escape, food, war experiences, food and more. The bombers from Deenethorpe all took off successfully and strained with their heavy loads to gain altitude. The 39 planes from the 401st Group were to form up after crossing the channel over northern France. Ninety B-17s from other groups that were part of the Eighth Air Force would be on their way to the target already. The bombers were to have fighter escorts over the entire mission. This kind of protection from the "little buddies" was critical to reducing the number of bombers lost due to enemy fighter attacks. The missions that went deep into German territory, such as this one to Weimar, were extremely dangerous prior to the arrival of the long range fighter, the famed P-51 Mustang, because the other major fighters — such as the P-47 Thunderbolt and my own twin-engine P-38 Lightning — did not have the fuel capacity and therefore the flying range of the P-51.

The German Air Force, the much-vaunted Luftwaffe, had been dealt a severe blow in the attacks on England when Hitler was planning to invade England in 1940. In the four years since that, and particularly in 1944 when the American presence in the air war became dominant, the Luftwaffe had continued to bleed. It was hampered by the effectiveness of repeated bombing attacks on aircraft factories, ball bearing plants and oil refineries, but also by increasingly losing their best and most experienced pilots in the vicious dogfights going on continually in the skies over Europe. But in August, 1944, they were down but far from out or defeated. They could still put up strong numbers with excellent aircraft and well-trained pilots.

Lt. Cain was nearing the assigned altitude of 20,000 feet when the German fighters attacked. They had learned of a gap in fighter escort coverage. When the bombers were still forming up into boxes of 12 bombers each and with fighter escort 5000 or 10,000 feet above them, they could be more easily attacked. Escorts may or may not be present and stragglers struggling to catch up and find their place in formations could be found and picked off. The Messerschmitt Bf 109s of the Luftwaffe fighter groups located in northern France spotted an opening and attacked. Soon three of the lumbering Boeing giants fell to the diving attackers with their powerful machine guns. Lt. Cain's "Carrie B II" was one of those which dropped out of formation, slowly rolling over and heading for the farmlands of the Dutch soil below. Seven parachutes emerged from the ill-fated bomber, including that of Second Lt. Cain and co-pilot Second Lt. Henderson. But Corporal Byers, the flight's Bombardier, and Ball Turret Gunner Sgt. R.E. Barron were killed. The seven who survived served out the war as Prisoners of War.

The two spares sent up in case of early mechanical problems had already returned to Deenethorpe along with one B-17 that had to abort because of mechanical problems. With the three downed bombers, the remaining 33 heavies from the 401st Group formed up and headed over the dappled countryside of occupied Europe.

It was a little after noon on that hot and humid August afternoon when I first heard a very distant rumble. We had already eaten our total ration for the day of cabbage-worm soup and black rye-sawdust bread. We knew with this kind of nutrition we needed to conserve our energy as much as possible. Our lives depended on not getting too weak from starvation. So we were sitting or lying in the hot sunshine on the pile of gravel and rocks we called home near the north end of Little Camp. The rumble had a familiar sound to it, but in these circumstances the familiar sounded vaguely wrong and disturbing. I turned over and saw some of the guys standing and looking up at the sky to the northwest.

"What is it?" I asked, although by this time I could guess myself.

"Sound's like Forts to me," said one, no doubt a B-17 crewman himself. The sound each aircraft made was distinctive, and we knew these sounds like I knew the spots on each cow back on the farm.

"Wonder where they are headed?" I asked casually.

"There they are!" someone shouted. "They're headed this way."

Most airliners these days fly at about 35,000 feet and they are barely visible specks, often seen at altitude only by the contrails. The bombers were flying at 20,000 feet, and we could see the contrails of the bombers clearly now, with little black specks in front of them. The formation they were flying in made them instantly recognizable, even if the planes were too far distant to clearly see — these were American B-17s, no doubt.

Then we noticed a single bomber ahead of the rest. That plane was nearly overhead. One of our group, a bombardier from one of our American bombers, was saying that it looked like a pathfinder. Pathfinders, created by the RAF, were elite crews developed for daylight bombing raids that dropped a flare bomb on a target, clearly marking it for the main force following.

"A bomb!" someone shouted, and suddenly we saw it. Dropping far below the pathfinder plane was a single bomb, and it was heading right for us. I mean right for us. I turned to run and saw my fellow prisoners trying to find a direction to run to. We were completely enclosed. Barracks to the west, electric barbed wire fence to the north and east and completely surrounding the camp. The bomb screamed down. We hit the dirt, covering our heads with our hands as best we could, each of us trying as hard as we could to make ourselves as flat and as small as we could. The bomb hit south of us, about a quarter mile away and smack dab into the German Armament Works. It was not a huge concussion and we could see the thick red smoke rising up into the still, humid air. It was the marker flare bomb, which explained the small explosion.

But, when we dared raise our heads again we saw many more bombers overhead. And then we saw their loads of 500-pound high explosive bombs coming down. I looked up, and I knew at that point that I was dead. In mere seconds there would be bombs falling all around us. I had seen enough from the air and from briefing photos of what damage these could do and always prayed I would never be under one. Now I was not only under one, but thousands, and they all seemed headed right for my head.

"Mother of God," I prayed, and I knew that in mere moments I would be in her presence. There was no doubt. We were flat as could be on the rocky ground we called home when the bombs hit. We could see nothing now as our eyes were closed as tight as we could make them, and our arms pressed our heads into the hard ground. But the concussions rocked me with such violence that I swore I was being picked up and thrown against the barracks. It started as one or two eruptions that seemed strong enough to rip our guts out of our bodies, but then rolled into an almost continuous explosion. I felt as if they were landing right on top of our group, and it seemed I was pushed and rocked from all directions at once. The debris was flying in all directions, and now I could feel things hitting my body.

What does it feel like to be dead? I thought. I was not afraid of pain, but now I was glad that this would be quick. The German guard was wrong. Looks like I'd leave here as wet dust sifting into the air. Still the explosions rocked, and the force of the concussion waves continued to beat on us as if we were in a typhoon. The heat from the explosions rolled over us in intense waves and was just one more element of the mix. I prayed to be welcomed into those holy gates but knew there was nothing more I could do to prepare. No last rites, no more confessions. What was done was done, and what would happen to me was determined. This story was over, of that there could be no doubt.

It seemed like hours that the explosions continued, occasionally slowing down and then starting again with a huge roar. Only once in awhile, when things seemed to have quieted down, did I lift my head and saw that my buddies were also lying with heads covered or peeking out cautiously. We would see another wave of bombers headed right for us and push our heads down again.

The different groups of bombers, of which the 401st was one, arrived in waves over Buchenwald and delivered their loads one box at a time. A total of 175 1000-pound high explosive bombs were dropped, plus 583 500-pound high explosive bombs. That is 466,500 pounds of explosives. But that was not all. After the high explosive bombs were released, the Allied planners followed this deadly barrage with incendiary bombs — 279 bombs, each 500 pounds of material designed to light and stoke huge fires, dropped after the high explosives. The strategy was more than effective. The targets were not only reduced to rubble, but now set ablaze to further wreak havoc. That makes a total of 605,000 pounds of destruction dropped for all intents and purposes on our very heads.

Finally, it stopped. We could smell the acrid smell of high explosives mixed with smoke of burning wood and equipment. We could hear the roar of the fire. For once, the fires and smells of the crematorium were overtaken by something much stronger. We slowly raised our heads. I wasn't certain at first if I was still alive, but after looking around I certainly hoped I was because if I wasn't, my sins had surely caught up with me. The hell I thought I was in when arriving here appeared to have turned out to be more reality than I thought. It was with increasing relief that I discovered I was still alive, and amazingly, so were all my fellows.

My respect for the skills of our bomber crews grew immensely that day. The targets were the two factories — one of which was at the edge of the enclosed camp. The other, Gustloff Works, was on the other side of the railroad station. Both of these factories were almost totally destroyed. There would be no further contribution from the slave labor of Buchenwald to the German war effort from these plants — they were knocked out for good. But there was more good news. The bombs had also landed on the SS barracks and officers' homes south of the camp's main gate. Remarkably, only as few as three bombs fell on any of the prisoner barracks and none on Little Camp, the northern part of the camp where we were located. We were within a quarter-mile of the bulk of the barrage, but not a single one of our number sustained any injuries — other than to our nerves, of course.

On August 27, the senior SS medical officer of Buchenwald sent a casualty report to his headquarters in Oranienburg. He reported 80 SS members were dead at that point, including 30 Buchenwald camp guards and 50 from the SS Transport Unit. There were 65 SS members missing, and 238 were reported in the hospital with injuries, including 75 SS and 163 others.

In addition, there were 24 family members or dependents of SS members who were also killed.

Five were reported dead from the Fichtenhain VIP Special Complex, with one missing and 37 wounded. As for prisoners, 315 were reported dead, 525 seriously wounded and 900 slightly wounded. The report was signed by SS Captain Schiedlausky, SS Medical Officer.

According to The Buchenwald Report, a total of 384 prisoners died with over 600 wounded. The prisoners killed and wounded were primarily working in the factories or in the notorious rock quarry. A bomb intended for SS housing had fallen on the quarry with devastating results on the prisoners. Although many of them in the factories escaped from the buildings in the early stages of the bombing or even prior to the first bombs hitting as a result of air raid warning, they had no place to go as the fence and sentry lines prevented them from leaving the area. It is not known how many of the prisoner casualties were from the very few bombs that landed on the barracks.

Among those killed in the attack was the wife and daughter of the camp's

Commandant Pister. Pister had replaced the extremely cruel Commandant Karl Koch in early 1942.

One special building was also destroyed by an American bomb. This was the Isolation Barracks, or so-called I Barracks. It was a large stone building across from the SS officers houses, surrounded by a 10-foot-high stockade and guarded continually by 12 SS men. This is where celebrity prisoners were kept and those the Germans did not want to mix with the rest of the prison population. Prominent prisoners held here included leading German politicians who had opposed Hitler, including Reichstag Deputy Rudi Breitscheid and his wife. Princess Mafalda, the daughter of the king of Italy, was held here, as was the former heads of government of France before that nation's fall to the Nazis. Members of the Stauffenberg family involved in the July plot to kill Hitler were held here, as were other German generals and leaders who had fallen foul of the Nazis. In the bombing, Breitscheid was killed and Princess Mafalda was severely wounded. Her arm was amputated by the same doctor who signed the above casualty report, but according to reports it was so badly botched that she died from loss of blood the next day. I Barracks was rebuilt and continued to host celebrity prisoners including Schussnigg, the former Chancellor of Austria, until the camp's liberation in April.

After the bombing, we just sat and tried to get ourselves calmed down. People react differently to such events and some were talking excitedly while others, like me, were mostly quiet, contemplating the experience of coming so perilously close to death. At first the conversations were mostly about the amazing display of bombing accuracy we had seen and how we had been the beneficiaries of the training and hard work that we ourselves had participated in such a short time before. But it wasn't long before a new thought occurred to us. What would our German captors think of us now, we Allied flyers? They could not take revenge or their anger out on the air crews above them who had dropped the deadly load. But, we were their compatriots. What might they do to us?

We did not have long to wait to find an answer to that question. In less than an hour after the bombing, and while the fires in the factories and SS housing were still raging, SS guards came into Little Camp in search of us. The ordered us to Roll Call Square. Not the other prisoners. Just us.

We looked at each other with deep concern. We formed into our units, as we had now become accustomed and marched toward the square. I was still shaking from the bombing and what I thought was certain death at the hands of my fellow American flyers, but now my legs felt weak and uncertain from an additional fear.

When we marched into Roll Call Square, it seemed our worst fears were to be realized. The MG-42 machine gun that was placed near the front of the square was fully manned. And they seemed serious and purposeful. We were instructed to line up. We stood at attention. My heart was pounding heavily, and again my thoughts went to my family, my all-too-short life, and the welcome I hoped I would receive in the next world. I expected the bullets to start flying any second as we stood and faced that machine gun. When they started, would I run? Yes, but where? There was no escape route. Running would result in bullets in my back or worse — whipping, beating and torture until I was dead and dragged into the crematorium. It was better to take the bullets in the front and hope they were mercifully quick and accurate. The German who greeted us as we came into camp was right. I would not leave here except as smoke.

The officer who stood in front and spoke to us was clearly furious. But instead of receiving the bullets from the machine gun, we were given orders to go into the factory building and help fight the fires. We were told to find anything that could be salvaged and take it out of the burning buildings. I felt immense relief — at first. Then I thought, how can I fight a fire with bare feet? We were not given any tools, or hoses, or any equipment. Just told to go into the buildings and salvage equipment and tools. A few of our group had been given wooden clogs that were like the Dutch wooden shoes. But most of us were barefoot. Still, it was better to go fight the fire than face the fire of the machine gun, and it appeared those were our options. Colonel Lamason gave the order and we marched as a unit past the crematorium toward the now destroyed German Armament Works.

With our bare feet and pajama-like uniforms, it seemed there was little we could do. We had no desire or intention to help out the German war cause in any way, so like many of the prisoners forced to work in the factory, we found ways to sabotage the effort. I went into a building that was only partially destroyed and found some machining equipment and tools that were undamaged. I picked up the heavy gear and made my way through the rubble back to the outside, as did several of my fellow prisoners. When we were outside, we looked at each other and I saw they had the same thought I did. No guards were around and we were the only prisoners forced to work in the salvage effort so we weren't afraid of kapos who would report our activities. I picked up the same heavy equipment and carried it back into the shop building. I would always be seen carrying something heavy and if it looked like I was going the wrong direction when spotted by a guard I could just pretend that I was maneuvering around the rubble.

And so we carried equipment for the next several hours. Pick something up, haul it outside with much show of exertion, then pick it up again and bring it back into the factory. Over and over and over. The work felt good and the almost meaningless effort to contribute to the damage caused by our fellow warriors from above gave our morale a huge boost. We continued the charade until we were called for the evening appell.

While we were busy at work "salvaging" equipment from the factory, the airfield at Deenethorpe began receiving the bombers it had sent off that morning. At 1548 hours, about 10 minutes to four that afternoon, the empty bombers with their tired crews returned. One after one they circled and then touched down on Runway 23. Eight planes suffered damage from the anti-aircraft barrages known as flak, four of them seriously damaged. But three B-17s did not return. Lt. Cain's Carrie B II was missing, along with "Down 'n Go" piloted by Lt. Finney and "Jill's Jalopy" piloted by Lt. Fish. Nine flight crewmen from the 401st died on that day bombing Buchenwald, and 18 more were added to the growing list of American Prisoners of War.

Appell that night was especially long as the camp commanders were trying hard to account for all of their missing, dead and wounded as well as the missing, dead and wounded prisoners. As we stood in the square while the sky darkened with the smoldering ruins of the Buchenwald, we waited patiently. We stood together, as stiff and military-like as our weakened and tired bodies would allow. We were Americans, and Britons, and Canadians, and Aussies and New Zealanders and more. We would win this fight. We might no longer be able to contribute much, but by God, we would do all we could. They could starve us, treat us like dogs, humiliate us and torture us, but they could not break our fighting spirits. And they could not take away our hope or love of freedom.

10 FILTH AND WORSE

After the excitement of the air raid died down, life settled into some form of normalcy in the area of Little Camp we called home. We ended up sleeping on the open, rocky ground for two weeks. At first it was very hot and the evenings were cool and comfortable, but as we headed into September, the night chill nearly overcame the increasing pain in our stomachs. We wondered if we were expected to spend the cold winter sleeping outside with no cover, only a thin blanket between three of us. We had little to no contact with other prisoners, as most sections were separated from each other with fences.

It was in the early days of our stay that Colonel Lamason, our Commanding Officer, made contact with Wing Commander F. F. Edward "Tommy" Yeo-Thomas. Destined to become one of the most famous and honored English war heroes whose exploits were featured in the book and movie titled "The White Rabbit," Yeo-Thomas was held in Buchenwald along with 36 British officers from S.O.E., or Special Operations Executive. This was a secret service and spy operation of the British, and Yeo-Thomas and his fellow officers had been captured behind enemy lines in civilian clothes actively working with the French Resistance to aid them in their fight against the occupiers. In fact, Yeo-Thomas made one of the greatest contributions to the war effort when after his first jump into France and subsequent return to England he sought and was given an audience with Prime Minister Churchill. Yeo-Thomas convinced the war leader to provide the French Resistance with the support and materials they needed to carry on the very dangerous but damaging fight against the occupiers of their native land.

After winning the support of the Prime Minister, Yeo-Thomas jumped again into France. He was captured and taken to Gestapo headquarters in Paris, the same place where I was interrogated. He, however, was subjected to the most brutal torture because they knew he had extensive knowledge of the French Resistance organization. For four days they beat him, subjected him to near drowning in ice-cold water with his feet and hands tied to such a degree that artificial respiration was used several times to revive him. His interrogators also employed one of their favorite tortures — electric shocks applied to the genitals. But he never broke and made two unsuccessful attempts to escape from the dreaded Compiegne prison, despite nearly losing his left arm from blood poisoning caused by the torture and his chains. They then sent him to Fresnes, where I was also held, and he arrived in Buchenwald from Fresnes just four days before we did. Yeo-Thomas was an absolute fighter and kept up non-stop efforts to escape. Shortly after arriving in Buchenwald, this courageous and hyperactive young man made contact with the main prison leaders of the camp who were anti-fascist communists and found out about the arrival of our group of Allied flyers. Stan Booker, one of our group, reported that Captain Christopher Burney and Wing Commander Yeo-Thomas both came into our camp and talked with Col. Lamason. Burney was also a captured S.O.E. officer and spent 18 months in Fresnes and another 18 months in Buchenwald, surviving with the help of other prisoners by hiding out in Block 46.

Thomas H. Blackham, a British officer who was part of our group, went with Col. Lamason to some of the meetings with Yeo-Thomas and reported that Lamason and "Dodkin," Yeo-Thomas' pseudonym to protect his identity, had known each other in England. This helped build the trust that was needed under the circumstances. Yeo-Thomas and Lamason met with the key anti-Nazi prison leaders, and it was through these meetings that Lamason determined to run our outfit as a military group so that we would be able to effectively aid the resistance if the SS decided to raze the camp to hide the evidence of their atrocities. It was through this contact with Yeo-Thomas that Col. Lamason discovered some very important and very disturbing information. The British and French special operatives knew that they were scheduled for execution. In fact, it wasn't long after they began meeting that 16 of the British officers were called to the main gate. The men were housed in Admission Block 17, and a call without warning to the gate meant either interrogation and torture or death. On September 10, just 20 days after our arrival, the call came and the men were led into the crematorium, which also contained a room with meat hooks installed against the walls. The ropes were tied tightly around their necks, and they were lifted onto the meat hooks to die. From there it was just a few short steps to the crematorium. Yeo-Thomas and Burney knew that their time was limited. But somehow, they also had information about our fate.

They knew that the instructions to the SS in Buchenwald from headquarters in Berlin was the same for us as it was for the S.O.E. officers. The justification for our planned murder came from the bureaucratic designation of our group not as enemy combatants but as "terrorfliegers," or terrorist airmen. On about May 20, 1944, Hitler decided that there were certain conditions under which American and English airmen who were shot down would be shot dead without court martial. These included firing at German airmen in parachutes, attacking German planes that had made emergency landings, attacking any public transportation and any low level attack on individuals. By this designation, and according to the unique logic of the German Fuehrer, we deserved the death penalty. But there were other possible reasons for this sentence as well. Prisoners of war who had escaped and were recaptured were subject to summary execution. But, when this happened, the authorities carrying out the order were to keep no record of their recapture so for official purposes the dead prisoners would be considered lost after their escape. What strikes one in these legal and bureaucratic maneuverings is the almost insane effort to keep some sense of order and even moral justification while carrying out the most inhuman, immoral and illegal activities.

I don't know if Col. Lamason knew the exact date of our planned execution at this time or not, but we would find out that it was October 24, 1944. He never revealed any information about his knowledge of our fate to any of us that we knew about, and it wasn't until many years later with the work of Art Kinnis and Stan Booker that we became aware of what the good Colonel had kept from us. According to Stan Booker, Phil Lamason spoke to 12 survivors of our ordeal at a POW convention in Hamilton, Ontario in 1983, and there explained that he knew the Gestapo had orders to execute us and that those orders had accompanied us from Fresnes. He said he did not reveal it to us at the time out of fear of what we might do that would jeopardize our position.

No doubt there was some German orderliness behind the schedule and the delays in executions of the English and French officers. On October 5, 1944, 21 more of the English and French officers were summoned and this time shot. That is, all but one — a Captain Harry Poole, known to the Gestapo by his French name, Peuleve. He managed an unlikely and daring escape.

Of the 38 captured French and English officers, Yeo-Thomas was one of the very few to survive the ordeal. With the help of prisoners working in the hospital, Yeo-Thomas took on the identity of a French prisoner who had died. With this switch the record showed that the Frenchman was still a prisoner but that Yeo-Thomas had died in the hospital. That is why his name and two others selected for the exchange were not on the list of those to be shot on October 5. The few remaining waited for their call to execution and one, Maurice Pertschuk, was hanged just a few days before the Allies liberated the camp. Captain Christopher Burney was one of four remaining English officers who survived to see liberation by hunkering down in an underground hiding place.

Col. Lamason told us about the execution of the 16 English officers on September 10, and life became even more grim. I kept thinking about what the guard had said when we first came into camp, about not leaving except as smoke through the chimney. When you are young, not quite 24 years old, all of life is ahead and it is not easy to face the likelihood of death. That's why they send young men and women to war; we think nothing bad can happen to us. Yes, it's very possible to be scared, but there is always this innate belief that everything is going to be alright. Now, despite our youth and optimism, we weren't so sure.

Our uncertainty and heavy dread grew along with our hunger and the long days in camp. Although we couldn't see a lot of the other prisoners except during appell, the horrors of this place became more and more evident. We even occasionally saw a large group of children. A total of 877 boys were kept in the camp at this time. The youngest that had been registered was three and a half, but many of them were between seven and 10 years old. The Jewish children had been taken away and shipped to other camps, there to receive the "final solution." Those who remained were being kept so the Germans could demonstrate the "protective custody" methods they undertook on behalf of the German people. Many of the prisoners we saw were starving, and we too started to take on the gaunt, empty, desperate look that we saw on so many faces when we first walked into camp. Our daily ration of cabbage or turnip soup laced with worms and one piece of black rye/sawdust bread was supplemented by a couple of boiled potatoes usually once or twice a week. The bread would swell up in your mouth after chewing it for a bit and so it helped make you feel like you were actually eating something, even though it contained a lot of sawdust that contributed no nourishment and couldn't be digested. The only other thing they provided was "coffee;" they called it coffee but it didn't even come close to tasting like coffee. It was usually served twice a day in our tin bowls, about five in the morning before appell and then again in the evening. Although we tried to preserve our energy, I could feel my body using up all its reserves and starting to eat into my muscles. The constant ache of hunger grew almost daily, along with a shaky weakness and pain from muscle loss.

Every day we saw bodies. Those who died during the night were taken out of their barracks and dumped outside the door so that kapos could pick them up and haul them to the crematorium. Frequently the bodies were stacked high outside the crematorium as the supply for its fires was greater than the capacity. Starvation was not the only cause of painful, agonizing death. Getting on the bad side of any kapo meant a severe beating or being sent to the punishment unit and work in the quarry. But it also often meant simply being beaten to death. Often the prisoner was simply kicked to death.

The punishment delivered on the whipping block visible to all of us during appell consisted of a prisoner being bent naked over the block and beaten on the back repeatedly with a cane. The prescription for this punishment called for it to be repeated after an interval of a few days, sometimes for an extended period of time. The treatment often left the prisoner in a condition that required hospitalization, and the peculiar treatment received in the hospital frequently meant death.

I never personally saw anyone killed, tortured or beaten to death. But several of our group did. And while I nor any of the other officers were ordered to do work in the camp, some of our enlisted group were forced to work in the quarry.

As I related earlier, many of us had become sick while on the train ride to Buchenwald. Nearly all of us suffered from dysentery, an infection of the gut caused by the filth all around us. The primary symptom of dysentery is diarrhea, but fever, severe cramps and vomiting are also often part of the fun. Not just diarrhea, but frequent diarrhea, and, pardon me, explosive, bloody diarrhea. That would be bad enough if it were not for the other conditions in place at the time, specifically the toilets.

There were no toilets. Instead there was a long concrete hole in the ground. It was about 20 feet long and about three feet wide. There was a little water running in the bottom but the sewage system at the camp had been built for 20,000 prisoners, and at the time we were there over 80,000 called it home — most of them with dysentery. So the contents of the hole tended to accumulate even though it was about seven feet deep. The concrete hole was ringed with a wall about two feet high and here is where we sat, leaning against a wooden rail that ran across the center of the pit. This "toilet" served a large number of prisoners from the blocks or barracks nearby, including those of us "camping" in the open air.

I mentioned the explosive nature of our illness, and this contributed significantly to the filth that surrounded us. There would be little warning for the eruption and all too often the results appeared before one had a chance to even sit down. This meant that to go to the "bathroom" we had to first wade through the muck. I am a farm boy from the Pacific Northwest and grew up taking care of a herd of big black and white Holstein dairy cows. Nowadays, these farms have lots of cement pads and farmers can keep the barns and the area surrounding the barns pretty clean. But in my day, the area outside the barn was nothing but dirt churned up by a herd of 40 or so cows waiting to come in for feed and milking. It rains a lot in the northwest, and the rain would turn this dirt, combined with the feces from all those impatient cows, into a special kind of smelly, sticky, clingy muck. It's the closest I can come to describing what it was like to have to go the bathroom. And remember, most of us, including me, had no shoes.

As soldiers, we did our best to keep at least one part of the toilet area clean. But, it was essentially hopeless. There were just too many sick men. For one of our group, getting through the muck to where he could sit down was only the beginning of his problems. While sitting there, leaning against the center rail, another prisoner in a great hurry approached the pit from the other side. He wheeled around to sit down but just a moment too late and the bloody, messy contents of his illness splattered all over the back of one of our flyers. There was a small faucet outside where we could rinse our feet or try to clean up a bit — remember — no showers or any bathing facilities at all. But the mess around the faucet did little to help in the clean up efforts.

An even worse experience happened to another of our group. While sitting on the wall on a dark night, he felt a tapping on his bottom from below. It was a Frenchman, a fellow prisoner who had the misfortune to fall into the seven-foot hole and needed a hand up to get out. In this case, it was an accident; but it is well documented that demented German guards used this same setup to torture and kill prisoners.

As for me, I felt luckier than most. When we entered camp we were given our prison uniforms without regard to size and I happened to get probably the biggest prison shirt made. When I put it on over my relatively small frame, it looked ridiculous, but it proved to be a Godsend. Obviously, the Germans didn't bother with providing us toilet paper or old Sears catalogs or even leaves. I discovered a very important use for all that extra fabric, and with care and gratitude applied a little at a time after my too frequent trips to the concrete hole. By the time we left Buchenwald, my shirt had been reduced to a rag that covered my neck and shoulders but little else. Good thing our stay was not longer.

It was not that our German captors had no regard for our health. Buchenwald is well known as the center for medical experiments conducted on prisoners, and it featured a remarkable collection of preserved body parts and skeletons used to "advance" German science and train physicians. The prisoners served as a "willing" source of "volunteers" for a wide range of medical experiments.

I still do not know to this day if I was a part of a medical experiment or just an unlucky recipient of the German idea of healthcare. But only a few days after we arrived we were ordered to a building. Such orders were met with great anxiety, because it was now clear that our lives meant nothing and we remembered with painful clarity the prediction of the welcoming guard about how we would leave this place. We stood in line and again by the groans of the men ahead of me I knew that what was about to happen would not be pleasant. A large syringe was filled with a bright green liquid and as we stood in front of the guard, it was jammed directly into our chest. Then it was extracted and without changing needles or even wiping it on anything to clean it off, it was jammed into the chest of the next patient.

When the German stabbed me with it, the obviously dull needle hit a rib bone. I nearly buckled under the pain. He attempted to pull the needle out but it was now buried into bone and was stuck. He pulled and turned and the needle broke off from the syringe, sticking out of my chest. He grabbed a needle nose pliers, clamped onto the needle, put a strong arm on my shoulder and yanked the needle out, tossing it to the ground. He fixed another needle on and proceeded to jab that one viciously into my chest again, this time missing bone. The same needle went into the next guy and the next until I saw him break it again.

Some reports from the studies done on Buchenwald after the war indicate that the Germans were inoculating prisoners to check the spread of typhus and other diseases. They may have done this because they were being overburdened with the dying and the crematorium simply couldn't keep up. Other reports indicate that such injections of prisoners were used to test highly toxic and experimental drugs for so-called medical research. It is known that for many prisoners this "preventive medicine" resulted in their deaths and exit from Buchenwald via the smelly chimney.

My introduction to the German healthcare system did little to improve my morale. We were all struggling to keep our hopes and spirits up, but often it was a futile effort. There seemed so little reason for hope. We knew that our families, the Red Cross, our military nor anyone else who cared had the slightest idea where we were. Even the Luftwaffe, or German Air Force, who should have been our caretakers didn't know what happened to us. We heard them say later that they knew we were in Paris in Fresnes, but after we left there they lost track of us — a nearly fatal mistake for us. When it became known to us that 16 English officers had been strung up in the crematorium on meat hooks, our despair hit new lows. It was very hard not to think as one woke up in the morning that this day might be our last, that we would get the dreaded summons and perhaps be subjected to unendurable pain on our way out to the next world.

For two weeks we continued to spend most of our time, including our sleeping time, in that little open corner of the camp. I'm not certain if Col. Lamason's protests finally took effect, but we were eventually told that we would move to a barracks. It was to be Block 54 in Little Camp, not far from where we had been staying. There was only one problem — Block 54 was already very full.

Each of the barracks held about 1000 prisoners. When I say "hold" I do not mean that there were sleeping accommodations or beds or bunks or anything like that. There were stacked wooden cubicles like you might see in a warehouse. Imagine three wooden crates stacked on top of each other. Each was eight feet long, four feet wide and four feet high. Each of these four-foot by four-foot spaces was the living and sleeping space for five. Fifteen men in a column 12 feet high and four feet wide. The barracks contained rows of these rough cubicles along both walls with a narrow center aisle — enough to hold about 1000 prisoners.

Our encouragement about finally getting a roof over our heads quickly turned to confusion. The barracks was full. The 877 kids kept in Buchenwald occupied Block 54, along with a few other prisoners. They were loud and active despite their extreme skinniness, and were a lot of trouble. Many had come from Eastern Europe and had seen the most atrocious events in their young lives. And many clearly did not share the same ideas about stealing as we did. So we moved in and quickly found that anything left laying around, such as our food bowls or blankets, would almost instantly disappear.

It wasn't long before we couldn't decide if living in the ridiculously overcrowded and tumultuous barracks was worse than braving the elements outside. No doubt Col. Lamason kept the prison leaders and German officers aware of our complaints and kept up a steady stream of protests against being treated as criminals or political prisoners instead of enemy combatants. Perhaps this helped our cause because after two and half days of sharing our living quarters with the children, they were ordered to take their meager belongings and leave.

We were finally left with something resembling peace and quiet. The barracks had a wood stove, and we discovered here that the sawdust bread could be made a little more palatable by sticking it against the hot stove until the wood in it smoldered and turned to charcoal. We also discovered something a little less pleasant. It did not take more than one night sleeping jammed together in our little cubicles to know that it was best to sleep on the top stack. The reason was simple. We slept with our heads sticking out toward the center aisle where there was a little air. There was no way to crawl up onto the upper "bunks" without stepping on the heads or shoulders or arms of the men on the lower bunks. It is one thing to have your head or face stepped on during the middle of the night, but when the reason for that journey out of the bunk was a quick trip to the concrete hole for the aforementioned purpose, that is quite another thing. Especially considering the condition of the area surrounding the concrete hole and the fact that the feet stepping on your head just came from there. Think muddy cow area and you get the picture.

I did everything I could to get to the top bunk — and tried like crazy not to step on my sleeping buddies below.

While we were very relieved to have the nearly 900 kids moved to another barracks, we couldn't help wonder what happened to them. When we didn't see them at appell anymore we became very concerned. Word soon came back that they had indeed left Buchenwald — as smoke from that horrid chimney. Every last one of them.

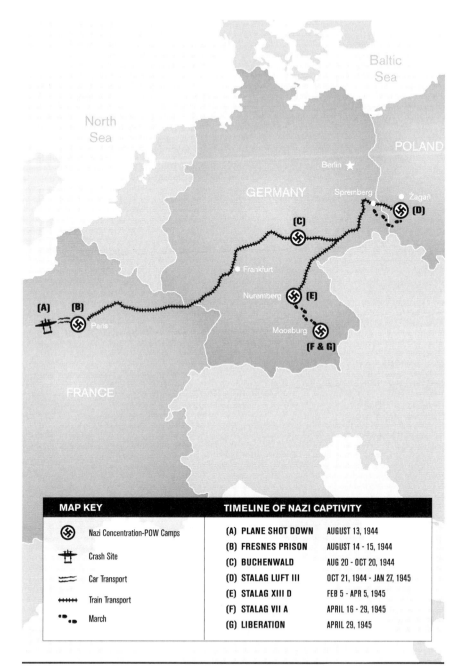

MAP KEY		TIMELINE OF NAZI CAPTIVITY	
⊛	Nazi Concentration-POW Camps	**(A) PLANE SHOT DOWN**	AUGUST 13, 1944
		(B) FRESNES PRISON	AUGUST 14 - 15, 1944
	Crash Site	**(C) BUCHENWALD**	AUG 20 - OCT 20, 1944
	Car Transport	**(D) STALAG LUFT III**	OCT 21, 1944 - JAN 27, 1945
	Train Transport	**(E) STALAG XIII D**	FEB 5 - APR 5, 1945
	March	**(F) STALAG VII A**	APRIL 16 - 29, 1945
		(G) LIBERATION	APRIL 29, 1945

Map of Nazi Germany illustrating Joe Moser's path from the site of his plane crash to Paris, Buchenwald, three POW camps, and finally to Moosburg, where he was liberated by U. S. forces on April 29, 1945.

Flight school graduation picture, class of 43-I.

Joseph Frank Moser, First Lieutenant United States Army Air Corps.

The American Lockheed P-38 Lightning - the fighter aircraft flown by Joe Moser during WWII. The P-38 had distinctive twin booms and a single, central nacelle containing the cockpit and armament.

"Group Loop Joe" poses during flight training school in Bakersfield, California.

Photo from "429th Fighter Squadron: The Retail Gang" by Karl Swindt.

Joe served in the 429th Fighter Squadron, which was created in Glendale, California on August 1, 1943. This photo was taken at Van Nuys Field, California. [Back Row] Thacker, Nolby, Banks, Cobb, Leahay and Kingston. [Front Row] Moser, unnamed mascot, McPherson.

.jrm

WAR DEPARTMENT

THE ADJUTANT GENERAL'S OFFICE

WASHINGTON 25, D. C.

IN REPLY REFER TO:
AG 201 Moser, Joseph F.
PC-N ETO171

1 September 1944

• Mrs. Mary P. Moser
1274 Northwest Road
Bellingham, Washington

Dear Mrs. Moser:

     This letter is to confirm my recent telegram in which you were regretfully informed that your son, First Lieutenant Joseph F. Moser, O-755,999, Air Corps, has been reported missing in action over France since 13 August 1944.

     I know that added distress is caused by failure to receive more information or details. Therefore, I wish to assure you that at any time additional information is received it will be transmitted to you without delay, and, if in the meantime no additional information is received, I will again communicate with you at the expiration of three months. Also it is the policy of the Commanding General of the Army Air Forces upon receipt of the "Missing Air Crew Report" to convey to you any details that might be contained in that report.

     The term "missing in action" is used only to indicate that the whereabouts or status of an individual is not immediately known. It is not intended to convey the impression that the case is closed. I wish to emphasize that every effort is exerted continuously to clear up the status of our personnel. Under war conditions this is a difficult task as you must readily realize. Experience has shown that many persons reported missing in action are subsequently reported as prisoners of war, but as this information is furnished by countries with which we are at war, the War Department is helpless to expedite such reports. However, in order to relieve financial worry, Congress has enacted legislation which continues in force the pay, allowances and allotments to dependents of personnel being carried in a missing status.

     Permit me to extend to you my heartfelt sympathy during this period of uncertainty.

Sincerely yours,

J. A. ULIO
Major General,
The Adjutant General.

This letter followed the initial telegram Joe's mother received that Joe was MIA. There was no further news of Joe until November 23, 1944.

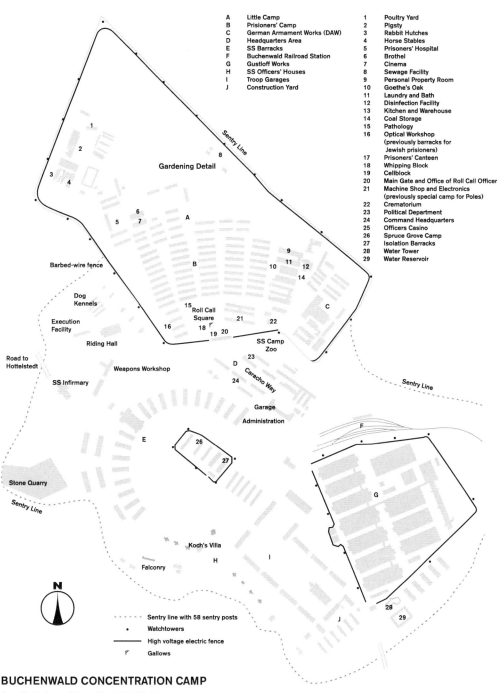

A   Little Camp
B   Prisioners' Camp
C   German Armament Works (DAW)
D   Headquarters Area
E   SS Barracks
F   Buchenwald Railroad Station
G   Gustloff Works
H   SS Officers' Houses
I   Troop Garages
J   Construction Yard

1   Poultry Yard
2   Pigsty
3   Rabbit Hutches
4   Horse Stables
5   Prisoners' Hospital
6   Brothel
7   Cinema
8   Sewage Facility
9   Personal Property Room
10 Goethe's Oak
11 Laundry and Bath
12 Disinfection Facility
13 Kitchen and Warehouse
14 Coal Storage
15 Pathology
16 Optical Workshop
      (previously barracks for
      Jewish prisioners)
17 Prisoners' Canteen
18 Whipping Block
19 Cellblock
20 Main Gate and Office of Roll Call Officer
21 Machine Shop and Electronics
      (previously special camp for Poles)
22 Crematorium
23 Political Department
24 Command Headquarters
25 Officers Casino
26 Spruce Grove Camp
27 Isolation Barracks
28 Water Tower
29 Water Reservoir

Sentry Line

Gardening Detail

Barbed-wire fence

Dog Kennels

Execution Facility

Road to Hottelstedt

SS Infirmary

Riding Hall

Weapons Workshop

Roll Call Square

SS Camp Zoo

Caracho Way

Garage

Administration

Sentry Line

Stone Quarry

Sentry Line

Koch's Villa

Falconry

N

- - - -   Sentry line with 58 sentry posts
•   Watchtowers
———   High voltage electric fence
Γ   Gallows

BUCHENWALD CONCENTRATION CAMP

from "The Buchenwald Report" by David A. Hackett

Photo from The Buchenwald National Memorial guide.

The entrance gate to Buchenwald bears the German phrase, "Jedem das Seine," which translates literally into "to each his own" but which means figuratively "everyone gets what he deserves."

Photo from 168 Jump into Hell: A True Story of Betrayed Allied Airmen by Arthur Booker and Stanley Kinnis.

Buchenwald was officially a work camp, so far fewer people were killed here than at other Nazi concentration camps. Nonetheless, 56,000 people died at Buchenwald, whether by work, torture, beatings or starvation. This picture shows prisoners at work; the camp's several factories together employed about 9000 prisoners at any given time.

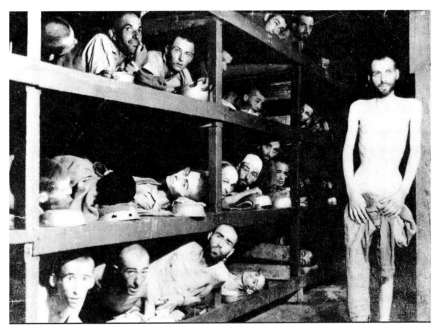

Photo from The Buchenwald National Memorial guide.

Overcrowded and incredibly unsanitary living conditions were the norm for prisoners of Buchenwald and concentration camps around Nazi Germany. Buchenwald was originally built to hold 6000 to 8000 prisoners. During Joe's stay in Buchenwald, the camp held over 80,000 prisoners including 168 Allied flyers.

Photo from The Buchenwald National Memorial guide.

Between July 1937 and April 1945, some 250,000 people were imprisoned at Buchenwald by the Nazi regime, including 168 Western Allies POWs and thousands of children.

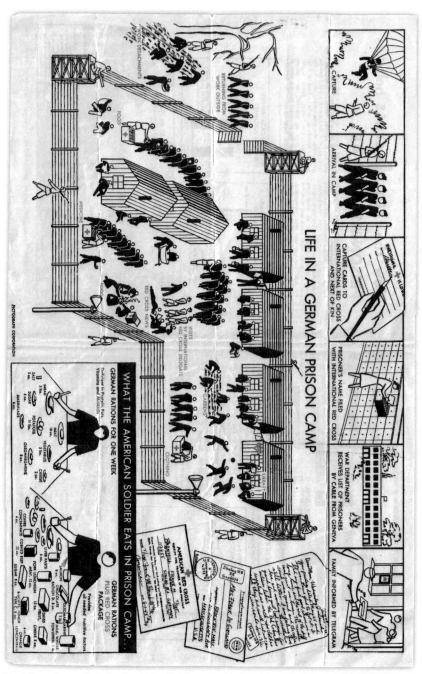

A Red Cross diagram illustrating the aid that Red Cross provided to prisoners in Germany's WWII POW camps.

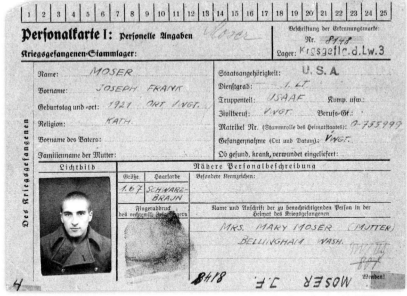

Joe's identification card from Stalag Luft III, the back of which indicates that Joe arrived to this POW camp directly from Buchenwald. The card was returned to Joe in the 1990s after being grabbed by a POW from the Gestapo office in Moosburg after Liberation.

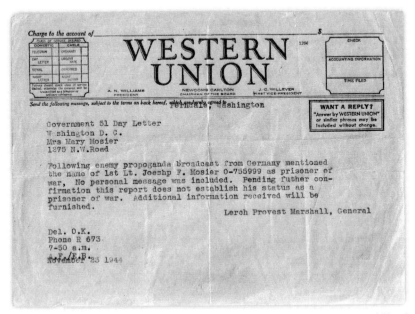

A telegram received by Joe's mother on November 23, 1944, informing her that Joe was no longer MIA and had been confirmed as a POW. This was the first hope they were offered that Joe was alive.

Photo taken from 168 Jump into Hell: A True Story of Betrayed Allied Airmen by Stanley Booker and Arthur Kinnis.

Here newly liberated prisoners of Buchenwald wait in stretchers as they receive care from U.S. soldiers. On April 11, 1945, over 21,000 prisoners were liberated from Buchenwald by the U.S. 83rd Infantry Division. Four days earlier, the Germans had forced thousands of prisoners to evacuate in anticipation of the advancing Allied armies.

Photo by Rosalee Divelbiss (Joe's sister).

Joe, Jim Hastin and an unidentified fellow prisoner stand outside one of Buchenwald's prisoner barracks during their 1993 visit.

Photo by Joe Moser.

Buchenwald's deathroom was located below the crematorium. It is estimated that around 1100 people died in this room. The room was complete with an elevator to transport victims upstairs to the ovens, a "body chute" for victims' remains, and hooks from which victims were hung to die (shown in this picture).

Photo by Joe Moser.

A modern-day view of Buchenwald's crematorium chimney, as seen from outside the camp's high, barbed-wire fence.

Photo by Joe Moser.

Buchenwald's crematorium contained six ovens, which are still on display to visitors today. It is said that almost 25% of Buchenwald prisoners died in the camp, most of whom were incinerated in these ovens.

This photo is from an article in the Bellingham Herald, November 11, 2001. Joe first told his story publicly in 1982 in an article in the Lynden Tribune. It was the first time his wife and family knew the details of what happened to him in WWII.

This photo appeared in the August 23, 1991, issue of Yakima Herald Republic, featuring (from left to right) Stan Paxton, Joe Moser, Jim Hastin and Art Kinnis. The group of four former aviators got together frequently to reminisce about their WWII experiences. In this picture, they stand before a 40/8 French boxcar at Sarg Hubbard Park in Yakima. This is the same type of boxcar that they rode in from Fresnes Prison to Buchenwald in August of 1944.

Joe and his wife, Jean, at a squadron reunion at the Space Needle in Seattle, July 4, 2000. Behind them is the 429th Fighter Squadron's emblem.

Back Row: Art Kinnis, Myles King, Phil Lamason, Jim Hastin **Front Row:** Don Leslie, unknown, unknown, Ed Carter-Edwards, Joe Moser

JOSEPH F. MOSER, O-755999, 1st Lieutenant, Air Corps, 474th Fighter Group. For extraordinary achievement in aerial flight. On 30 July 1944 Lt MOSER despite heavy enemy ground fire successfully led his squadron on a bombing attack directed at cutting the enemy supply lines and transportation, and contributed in great measure to the damage and destruction inflicted on supplies vitally needed by the enemy. Lt MOSER successfully destroyed two locomotives and ten fright cars; while with repeated strafing passes, he damaged two antiaircraft positions and thus enabled his squadron to complete its mission unimpeded. The great loss inflicted on the enemy contributed greatly to the success of allied ground forces. Entered military service from Washington.

An excerpt from an official document dated June 22, 1945 and issued from the Ninth Air Force Headquarters, which grants Joseph F. Moser the Distinguished-Flying Cross Award. This document was discovered in Air Force archives at the end of 2008. In January 2009, officials of the McChord Air Force base presented to Joe his lost Distinguished-Flying Cross.

Photos by Gabriel Rodriguez.

Over a period of two years, Joe Moser told his story to Gerald Baron (author). Here the two are pictured reviewing sources together in Joe's Ferndale, WA, house in early 2008.

Photos by Gabriel Rodriguez.

Joseph F. Moser, 2008.

11 RESCUE

My shirt was getting shorter and shorter. The days were also getting shorter, darker and colder. We could now imagine what early morning appell in our filthy pajama-like prison uniforms would feel like, barefoot and in the snow. Like my fellows and the other some 80,000 prisoners here in Buchenwald, the lack of nourishment had sapped my body of strength. I was now down to under 120 pounds from my normal at this time of my life of 155 pounds. I would get to 113 pounds before leaving. I was now one of those empty human sacks, eyes staring out lifelessly behind deep sockets with sunken cheeks and the filthy striped uniform sagging over my skeleton.

But I and 165 others in our group of 168 were still alive. Two had died in the prison's dangerous hospital. They were British flyer Philip Hemmens and Lt. Levitt Clinton Beck. Beck was a fellow American fighter pilot who had been shot down and was held by the French underground for several months before being betrayed by the same "Jacque" who had betrayed most of our group into Gestapo hands. In off-times during his fighting career and then during his months of captivity, Beck wrote of his experiences as a fighter pilot and the manuscript along with a number of letters to his mother were miraculously shepherded through the French and Red Cross bureaucracy and received by his family. The manuscript was published under the title "Fighter Pilot," and is still in print and available. Several others of our group were in the hospital at one time or another, including Joseph Sonshine and Roy Allen. Allen, a B-17 pilot, became well known in the last few years for his experiences, which were featured in a 2004 History Channel documentary called "Shot From the Sky." I was one of the survivors interviewed for that documentary.

Beck died in the main hospital from pneumonia. Allen also suffered from pneumonia and got to the infirmary before Beck. This was fortunate for Allen, because when Beck arrived at the infirmary, there was no more room, and the move to the main hospital — intended for SS use — was in effect a death sentence. Not that recovering in the infirmary was a piece of cake. Allen reports that the main kapo would come through and decide who had been there too long or whom he had taken a dislike to and would nod at them, saying "crematorium." They would usually be given a pill or a needle and would be dead in a couple of hours. Others were not so fortunate. Allen reports seeing patients dumped in a barrel of ice cold water, then wrapped in a rubber sheet and left to die. Pneumonia was certain after such treatment, and a suffocating death was not long in coming.

As weak as I was, I was still on my feet. Life was now more or less routine. Appell at five in the morning. Supposed "coffee" for breakfast, cabbage and worm soup with bread at noon, "coffee" again in the evening. Two appells a day — sometimes only for an hour or so each time, sometimes for hours standing in the cold. Sometimes "entertained" by screaming, moaning victims on the whipping block.

Roy Allen reports seeing a scaffold with six nooses used continually for disposing of Russian prisoners of war. But we would find out later that the Germans had devised a far more efficient means of disposing of their Russian prisoners. And it was in this case in particular that Buchenwald went beyond a work camp for criminals and political prisoners to a true death camp. In a building that had previously been a horse stable outside the main fence to the west of the main camp, they created an execution facility. The murderers had devised a way to quickly dispose of the prisoners by telling them to undress in an outer room, that they were going to be disinfected in a bath. The naked men were led into a small room with a radio blaring loudly to cover the sounds of the execution. They were placed against a wall with a small hole in the back and a sliding platform that came down flat on their head. This aligned the hole directly in line with the prisoner's neck, and a rifle held by an executioner in the next room was shot directly into the back of the neck. The prisoner was then dragged from the room into a waiting truck for the short ride to the crematorium. The showers in the room were turned on to wash the blood away and the next prisoner was brought in. Soon this was not a fast enough method, and groups of the unfortunates were brought into the soundproof room and shot with pistols. Five hundred Russian soldiers a day were killed between the work hours of 9 p.m. and 5 a.m.

While we continued to hope that Lamason or someone would find a way out of this situation, the days dragged into weeks and our hope became harder and harder to cling to. It became almost impossible after receiving word first on September 10 of the execution of the 16 British and French officers caught as spies, and then of most of the rest of them on October 5. Our days were spent quietly, spent often playing bridge with homemade cards made from scraps of cardboard, with our thoughts focused much of the time on the pain that accompanied starvation. It is hard to take your mind off food when you are continually and desperately hungry. Hope and hunger do battle in this environment, with extreme hunger and fear picking away at what little hope remains to keep spirits alive. I do not think I ever really gave up hope, but there were times when it seemed futile to hope — times I felt ready, even eager, to go to the next world. In those times, thoughts about home, about my mother and brother and sisters, plus all that wonderful food kept me wanting to see yet another day. But realizing that they had no idea where I was, whether I was alive or not and that they would likely never know what happened to me, caused me pain that was often greater than the pain of my body screaming out for nourishment.

Our marching as a unit back and forth from appell helped us to remember that we might be filthy, starving skeletons, but we were still soldiers in the greatest unified military organization in the history of the world. We believed that while we might not see the day itself, we had no doubt that the outcome of this great struggle was certain and that the world would be freed from the unbelievable nightmare of Nazi control.

I do not know exactly how our rescue came about. I do know that the Luftwaffe was aware that the SS held a group of Allied flyers and that they were not happy about that. There were battles going on in Berlin for control of our group between the Luftwaffe and the SS leadership that we were not aware of. We found out that the Luftwaffe knew about our existence while in Fresnes but had lost track of us when we were put on the train with the French resistance prisoners. They were trying to find us, but it was far from certain whether they could do so in time and whether they would have the ability to rescue us. Our execution was scheduled for October 24, as we found out later. If they did not find us before then and if they did not prevail on whoever would make the decision in Berlin to release us to Luftwaffe custody, it would be too late.

It might strike today's reader as unusual that there would be Germans in Hitler's military who would fight to save us from execution. The reason such a question would even occur is that we have come to see the history of this regime in terms of complete black and white. This is far from the truth. Even in Buchenwald, there was evidence of good people caught in overwhelming and horrible circumstances. Being a member even of the SS did not automatically make one a cruel and animalistic human being. Within Germany, many of those fighting mightily for the German cause did not abandon their morality, their ideas of right and wrong and their concern about doing things according to international law and the basic human ideas of how to treat people. The fact that a great many people did does not say so much about the German people, but much more about our basic human condition. It is frightening to think about how close each of us is to leaving our moral nature behind in the circumstances of fear, hatred and hostility. It may surprise some, but to this day I have no bitterness or anger or bad feelings about the German people, or even the people who were responsible for my suffering.

There is no doubt in my mind that many in the Luftwaffe did not approve of the SS treatment of prisoners in general, and particularly of their treatment of enemy flyers. In World War I there was a strong bond between pilots on both sides of the conflict so that Allied pilots mourned the death of Baron von Richthofen, the German ace and greatest pilot who had killed so many of their fellow pilots. That bond was largely gone in World War II, but there still remained a fraternity of fellow flyers.

I am not certain if the Luftwaffe found out about us from the connections that Yeo-Thomas and Christopher Burney had or if they found out through the contact made by Joseph Sonshine while he was in the infirmary. Sonshine was seriously ill with an abscess on his left elbow that was caused by an injury from bailing out of his plane. His health was further weakened by diphtheria, malnutrition and a back injury. He reported in Kinnis' and Booker's book that while in the hospital he was visited by a Luftwaffe doctor. He was asked why he was in a concentration camp instead of a POW camp. One thing is certain, Col. Lamason never let an opportunity pass by where he didn't make it clear that we strenuously objected to our treatment and that our tormentors were violating the Geneva Convention.

None of our group has been able to find out what happened in Berlin regarding our status. All we know is that one day, October 12 and just a few days after the 21 English and French officers were shot, the camp received a visit by high ranking Luftwaffe officers. They were escorted to our barracks and there several in our group, including Col. Lamason talked with them. The disgust they felt for their fellow German SS officers was clear. It was also certain that they did not approve of the way we were being treated and the conditions of the camp. They left and we felt some renewed hope, but even that was mixed with the realization that we remained in the hands of the SS and that anything might happen. The Luftwaffe officers made no promises of rescue, but the fact that someone knew we were there and didn't like the situation was encouraging to us. We almost dared to hope again, but a "Job" kind of hope where you fear that too much hope will bring a catastrophe on yourself.

On October 20, after morning appell, SS guards appeared at our barracks and ordered us to gather our belongings and report to the warehouse building. Of course, this caused an immediate increase in our blood pressure as such a summons at Buchenwald was a virtual death sentence. I remembered again the warning we received when entering, that the only way we would leave this place was as smoke through the chimney — the smelly, dirty, horrible chimney that never stopped spewing dark, choking, acrid smoke. We formed up outside our barracks, then marched as a unit, uncertain of our fate, but with the sense that finally one way or another it would be decided very soon.

We entered the storehouse building where the Germans with their typical orderliness and efficiency had neatly stored all the personal belongings of the prisoners. I couldn't believe it when I was handed the same clothes I had been wearing when I first entered Buchenwald. I even received my shoe with the torn-off toe. It felt unbelievably good to see those clothes and that shoe again — perhaps it was a reminder that I had been through many close calls and that somehow I was still here. We were pretty certain that if they were going to cremate us, they wouldn't bother to give us our clothes back only to take them away again. There were smiles on our skeletal faces — big smiles. I knew deep in my heart that my mother's and family's prayers were being heard and that I was being watched after by Someone far more powerful and more merciful than these Germans.

Still, we hardly dared breathe, hardly dared hope too much, even when we were marched back to the railroad station past the crematorium, past the main gate, past the bombed-out factories. I saw again the emaciated faces, the hungry, empty stares. I looked back at them with a deeper understanding of their pain and suffering than I could have imagined just two months earlier. We had been in this place exactly two months, and now it looked — dare we hope — that we were leaving, and not as smoke through the chimney.

We saw the now familiar "40 and 8" boxcars lined up behind the engine. Oh no, not this again, I thought. But this time they put only about 35 or 40 of us in each car. That seemed positively comfortable compared to the 95 who had been jammed into my car on the way into Buchenwald. As it turned out, we could have used a few more, because unlike the first sweltering August ride, the weather had turned cold. Even though we had our own clothes back, we were chilled to the bone and needed to hang close to each other to keep warm enough on the two-day boxcar ride.

Even though it was the typical German transportation treatment, we had been freed from the nightmare of Buchenwald. Little to no food to ease our extreme hunger — now I was down to 113 pounds. A five-gallon bucket for water and another five-gallon bucket for a toilet. The air was close because the only ventilation came from those barbed wire-covered areas at two corners — the same small hole that had cost that French boy his life over two months earlier. With 40 men who had not showered or bathed in over two months and who had endured the most filthy, foul conditions imaginable, the air quickly became hard to breathe. But I certainly was not complaining, because once out of wind range of Buchenwald, the everlasting smell from the crematorium was finally behind me. So we grouped tightly together, sitting or standing huddled for warmth and support, prepared for the long and uncertain ride ahead.

Our future was far from certain, but it is possible that there were few people in this war or perhaps any war who looked more forward to a POW camp than our group. If that is indeed where we were heading, and it was our fondest hope — we were certain that conditions would be better where we were heading, particularly when we saw the disgust exhibited by the Luftwaffe officers on their visit. It seems ironic now, but the Luftwaffe men who accompanied us as guards seemed our saviors. We wanted desperately to be free from the Gestapo and the SS and to be in the hands of men who still honored the brotherhood of fellow aviators, despite the bloodiness and brutality of the conflict we were both engaged in. The continual fear of beatings, torture, death by disease and starvation, we began to slowly let go. Even more important, we knew that once in a POW camp, our families would know we existed; our units would receive word that we were no longer MIA but had been found. With the Luftwaffe finding us, I dared hope that my family would soon know that I was alive and might even know where I was. It is hard to describe the feeling of being so far away from family and realizing they don't know whether you are dead or alive or where in the world you may be. It is a special kind of loneliness.

It slowly dawned on me that maybe there would be a reality to my life again. In the empty abyss that was Buchenwald, to a large degree I felt we had disappeared from the face of the earth. It seems a little like that question of whether a tree falling in the forest makes a sound if there is no one there to hear it. Were we really alive and part of this earthly existence if we had completely disappeared? Does life matter or have any meaning if no evidence of your presence exists? Now we were freed from that. We were alive and filled with hope and had a zest for life that had largely been missing for those two months. It was a little like a re-birth, like being born again, and that is how I felt riding away from those horrors on the train that day. I'm certain my feelings were shared by those who shared that ride with me.

I would find out later how difficult those days were for my family. They received word by telegram that I was Missing In Action. I still have the telegram that my mother received at 1274 Northwest Road, time-stamped 3:25 p.m. on August 31, 1944. But, then no word. Nothing. The longer that silence goes on, the more likely of course that the flyer and loved one would not be found alive. There was a normal and expected time between capture and when the Red Cross would be informed of the arrival of the prisoner in a POW camp. But in our case, that expected time passed without word from the Red Cross. The conclusion to be drawn was too obvious, and the longer the delay the more clear the result. Jim Hastin and I talked on the train about what receiving word of our situation would mean to our families. My heart felt lighter than I had ever thought possible — a strange sensation for someone heading to a place thought by most flyers to be worse than hell. If they only knew.

No one told us where we were headed. Finally, in the late afternoon on October 22, 1944, the train came to a grinding, huffing stop. After a while, the heavy wooden doors of the cattle car were pushed open and we could smell fresh air again. It was almost exactly two days after leaving Buchenwald, and we had no idea where we were. Our starving bodies were cramped and stiff from the two days of bouncing on the rough wooden floor, and we gingerly jumped from the train, most of us sitting on the edge at the door to get off like old men rather than jumping with a springy bounce as we would if we were still the 24 year old boys that our ages said we were.

Now we could see a fence, guard towers, barracks buildings. But this was different. There was a different air about it, an orderliness, a sense of caring and purposefulness that was lacking in even the quickest glance at Buchenwald. We did not know what this was called, but it sure as heck looked like a POW camp. We were brought immediately into the main administrative building through the main gate. There again, everything seemed efficient, neat and orderly. We were handed a set of clothes and, after removing my soiled uniform one last time, I said goodbye to my toeless shoe, never to see it again. What I wouldn't give for that souvenir now. But the clothes we were given were winter clothes, including a heavy wool coat and good high-top shoes. This was not Buchenwald. My spirit felt lighter and lighter the more certain I became that this is where we would remain.

Indeed, we had arrived at Stalag Luft III, our home for the next six months. Built as a camp specifically for Air Force officers, Stalag Luft III was seen as a model POW camp. You certainly wouldn't get an argument about that from us! It seemed we had checked into a Hilton after our time at Buchenwald. It was located in Sagan, about 70 miles as the crow flies southeast of Berlin. Sagan is now the Polish city of Zagan.

After receiving our new clothes, we were immediately put in a line to have our identification photos taken. Again, the efficiency of the German system was amazing, even though it was getting to be late in a war that was quickly going very badly for the Nazi regime. Still, the organization and detail never wavered. My photo was taken, and my identification card was written up in neat German script with the photo attached. It showed my nice new and warm German-issued winter coat. It contained my mother's name and city where she lived, "Bellingham, Wash." It had my height, hair color and 13 separate items of personal description. It also indicated that I arrived from "K. L. Buchenwald." K.L for Konzentration Lager or Concentration Camp Buchenwald. How I would have loved to have had this card in my possession later while being interrogated on two separate occasions regarding my release from active duty by Air Force officers who clearly did not believe my story about being held in Buchenwald. What is truly amazing is that I have this identification card today. That in itself is a testament to German order, because when we were ordered out of Stalag Luft III with the Russian artillery audible in the distance, the Luftwaffe guards gathered up all our identification cards and carried them to our next destination. Then we were moved again, and again our identities came with us.

When we were liberated in April of 1945, one of my fellow Buchenwald prisoners went into the town of Moosburg, which was the town nearest our final destination in German hands. For reasons I will never know, he went into the Gestapo headquarters in the town and came across the files of POW identification cards. He grabbed some of these cards on his way out and carried them back with him home. Forty-nine years later, he began searching for the owners of these cards. My card found its way back to me in Ferndale through Jim Hastin in 1993 and is now one of my most prized possessions.

After the administrative processing was done, we were accompanied to our new homes. Our Buchenwald group would not stay together. We were just assigned barracks rooms according to where there were openings. I was sent to the barrack identified as Block 104 in the North Camp. Jim Hastin was sent to Block 112, which was fairly close by and I continued to see him often. As it turned out, Block 104 was the most famous barracks of the entire war in the most famous POW camp of the entire war, and possibly any war — and certainly not because I lived there! It was in this very barracks, underneath the very stove on which I helped cook my meals for the next several months, that the tunnel called "Harry" was started. This is the tunnel from which 76 Allied airmen escaped on March 24, 1944. "The Great Escape," as it became known, is recognized as one of the most famous escapes in history. It set a world record for mass escapes from a POW camp and was the subject of one of the most famous and loved movies in U.S. movie history. Sadly, the story ended with only three of the 76 successfully eluding the massive manhunt that scoured the countryside around Sagan for days following the escape. On the direct orders of Adolph Hitler and to the shock and horror of not just the Allies, but the Luftwaffe as well, and in direct violation of the Geneva Convention, 50 of those who escaped, including the leader Roger Bushell, were shot by the Gestapo. Their cremated remains were delivered back to the camp and were buried with full military honors in the camp cemetery.

Block 104 was my new home, and a very different place than Buchenwald. That night I settled into my own bunk — I didn't have to share with four other stinky fellows in a four-foot-wide wooden mattress-less sleeping box in quarters so tight that if any turned we all had to turn at once. And, best of all, there was real food! I swear I was the happiest and most content man in all of Germany.

12 A POW AT LAST

I met my new roommates when I first entered my assigned bunk room in Block 104. It was evening, and I was exhausted and hungry. The first thing I really noticed was my bunk. Yes, a real bed — wooden bunks built stacked in twos, with eight in a room that was not much larger than a college dorm. But it was a bed! With a mattress! Well, yes, the mattress was made of straw, and I would soon discover like the rest that the straw made a cozy home for thousands of little critters, many of them having an appetite for human blood. But it was a bed, and I had not seen a bed of my own since August 13, nine weeks earlier.

I shook hands with my six new roommates and just couldn't get used to how they looked. I mean, they looked like real human beings. Certainly not overly fed, but they were clean, shaven and did not smell of the filth of diarrhea and dysentery. Most noticeably, they didn't have that empty, sunken, defeated stare that we had become accustomed to seeing on every face, including our own, at Buchenwald. Extreme hunger combined with hopeless despair and animalistic treatment quickly saps the very essence of what it means to be a human being. Unless you have experienced that degree of physical and emotional suffering, it's hard to imagine it in others — but it is instantly recognizable in another face if you have suffered in this way. It is hard for me to imagine anyone going through Buchenwald and not coming out with an almost infinite level of empathy and sensitivity to those who suffer to the extremes in body, mind and soul.

They looked back at me as they warmly welcomed me and shook my hand, and as they did I recognized their quiet, fearful, questioning look. "What is that we see in you?" they seemed to say. It frightened me a little to think that I too had lost a sense of the meaning of being human and that it was something they immediately saw. I wondered for a moment if I would ever get the spark of real life back in my eyes.

Four of my roommates were Polish, and two were Americans. All, of course, were flyers, and I believe all were officers. Stalag Luft III was built specifically for Allied air officers, and there were relatively few enlisted men. That included most of the enlisted men who were with us in Buchenwald who were sent to other Luftwaffe POW camps. The Kriegie log from South Camp showed that on October 21, 25 sergeants from Buchenwald arrived in camp, so at least some of the enlisted men were assigned to the camp. Stalag Luft III was intended by the Germans to be a show camp in its enlightened treatment of Allied POWs, and in many ways it lived up to that attempt. To us it seemed like a country club. But after the well-publicized mass escape and the subsequent cold-blooded murder of the officers, Stalag Luft III became much more well known in the U.S. and Allied nations. It became one of the greatest examples of the German leadership flaunting the Geneva Convention in show, but not in practice.

It is one of my great regrets from these days that I do not recall the names of my new roommates and that I lost all contact with them after the war. I attribute this mostly to the decision I made after the war, for reasons I will explain later, to not talk about my experiences and assign the whole of my war experiences to the dustbin of my memory. I do remember my roommates very fondly and with deep gratitude, which again will be explained later. The Poles spoke passable English, and they had been fighting with the RAF when they were shot down. One was a fighter pilot, and the other three were bomber crews. The Polish flyers had been there almost from the time the camp was built in early 1942. I think they had been prisoners before the construction of this camp, because as I recall they had been POWs for almost four years. The Kriegie life had become just their way of living. POWs called themselves "Kriegies" after the German word for Prisoner of War, "kriegsgefangener," which proved too burdensome to pronounce.

The two Americans were both fighter pilots — P-47 jockeys, as I recall. All of us immediately had a bond that comes with being pilots and having stories to share about harrowing and humorous experiences. But the time for story telling would come later. In the meantime, I was starving and tired to my very bones. My roommates generously gave me some of their spare food that first night. I was careful and only ate a little. Many of my fellow Buchenwalders were not so careful and grew sick off the generosity of their block and roommates in the next few days. It is now well known that it is a big mistake to give a starving person a lot of food, particularly rich food, because it will further disrupt the digestive system. Many who survived Buchenwald and the other death and work camps died in the days following liberation until prisoners' food intake became strictly controlled by medical staff who were part of the liberation force. It is sad to think of this additional suffering and death caused by the very people who wished nothing more then to help them and ease their starving bodies.

I rolled into bed that first night with some food in my empty stomach, into what seemed at the time a feather-soft mattress, and in the company of fellow flyers. I crawled into my bunk with my new warm German-issued winter clothes and slept like a teenager. We were guarded now by Luftwaffe guards instead of SS guards, and while the change was not obvious in our induction into camp, it would soon become obvious in how we were treated and in the relationships between guards and prisoners. For the first time in two months, I did not have to worry about someone's feces-sodden foot coming down on my head in the middle of the night. Nor did I have to worry any longer about running out of shirt to deal with my continuing dysentery discomfort. I slept very well indeed.

My new routine of life as a Kriegie began the next morning. It became obvious quite quickly that while my roommates were sympathetic to my condition, they did not believe what I told them about Buchenwald. The same was happening all around the camp as my fellow Buchenwalders related the tales of what they had seen and experienced. It was simply beyond what the POWs could conceive of, in part because they too were living as prisoners under German care. In contrast to what they heard from us, their life was reasonably acceptable, even comfortable to some degree. It didn't make sense, given the complete ignorance of essentially all the world at that time of what human beings were capable of in that special creation known as a concentration camp. It didn't square with anything they knew of German treatment or of life itself, and so we all had a hard time getting anyone to believe us. The log entry of the POWs in South camp said in parentheses about those arriving from Buchenwald: "Kriegies learned that things were rougher all over." Perhaps part of the reason for the disbelief is that the POWs did really think that their experience of hunger and discomfort was about as bad as it could get and resisted the idea that their situation was pretty good compared to others. This disbelief was deeply frustrating to many of our group, and the bitterness that is still felt by some about this is clear in the way they have relayed the stories of their introduction into the various POW camps.

This same disbelief continued for me and for many others much beyond the initial days at Stalag Luft III. The Air Force officers who debriefed me on my discharge similarly doubted my account, as did some I spoke to at home after the war. It has not been the burden to me that it was to some, but I can remember feeling frustrated that after having gone through all that and then arriving at this place, a real POW camp, that what we said should be counted for so little. It took days of the Kriegies getting together who had talked to individual members of our group alone before they began to accept that this was not some big conspiracy that we had hatched to deceive them. Certainly our starving physical condition did much to convince them, as did the sickness many of our group suffered as a result of eating too much immediately after arriving. The sheer filthiness of our bodies, despite the clean clothes we had been provided, gave further evidence.

Freezing cold showers were once a week. I can't recall when my first one was, but washing off two months of fear, sweat, feces and the grime of traveling and living in such close proximity to other prisoners felt like a baptism. Now I began to feel whole again, a human being worthy of the company of other human beings.

I was awakened that first morning with the word "Appell!" That at least was familiar to me. We dressed quickly and headed for Appell Platz, the roll call square where all prisoners from that section of the camp were marched and stood at attention until everyone was counted. As in Buchenwald, the twice-a-day roll call was the primary means by which the German guards determined that there had been no escapes. If the numbers weren't right for whatever reason, we stood there until the accounting was complete and any questions resolved. If the numbers were off in the morning appell, it was usually because some Kriegie was sleeping soundly and his roommates had neglected to pull him from out of the covers in their own haste for appell.

Sometimes the count took hours, the same as in Buchenwald. Now at least we had warmer clothes and did not have machine guns pointing at us nor a gallows to look at.

Stalag Luft III was divided into five separate camps of about 2000 each. The entire camp was 60 acres and held about 10,000 prisoners. There were five sections — North Camp, South Camp, East Camp, Center Camp and West Camp, plus a large German headquarters area and guard quarters area that was at least as large as the North camp where I was located. Barbed wire fencing prevented crossing from one camp to the other so each was largely run as an independent POW camp. There was a fairly large open area of about 15 acres between South camp and North camp. Block 104 was in the middle and at the northernmost boundary of the entire camp, which is one reason it was selected by the escape planners for the primary escape tunnel. From under the stove in my barracks, it extended over 300 feet, the length of a football field, underneath the barbed wire and guard towers into the woods to the north. The tunnel ended up a little short of the woods, which proved to be a key factor in the discovery of the escaping prisoners. Jim Hastin was housed nearby in Block 112, while Art Kinnis ended up in West camp.

The entire camp was, of course, surrounded by electric barbed wire fencing with guard towers located about 100 yards from each other along the lines of the outer fence. When the guards were spooked, particularly during the frequent air raid sirens, they would sometimes fire directly into the barracks. A Corporal Miles from South camp was shot and killed in one of these unwarranted shootings. Ten yards inside the main perimeter fence was another single-strand warning barbed wire fence. This represented the outer limits that we could walk, because if you stepped inside that 30-foot separation area, you would immediately attract the attention of the guards. And, given the right circumstances, this kind of attention could be fatal. So that thin strand of steel became the boundary of our existence; it was along this fence we would walk and run for exercise once our strength began to return. It was also where conversations could be held without fear of being overheard by the "ferrets," the English-speaking guards who intermingled with the Kriegies in hopes of finding out about tunnels, escape attempts or other nefarious activities.

Of course, the best piece of news I discovered in that first day in POW camp was the food situation. I should make it clear that the food was probably the greatest item of complaint among all Kriegies, other than being behind barbed wire to begin with. And it is true that compared with the incredible riches of our daily fare that we all take for granted, the Kriegie food was pitiful. But compared to what we had become accustomed to, it couldn't have been much better if it had been served by Mr. Hilton or Mr. Marriott themselves. The "goons," as the German guards were universally referred to by Kriegies, provided a weekly ration per prisoner of one loaf of army bread (now minus the sawdust), 400 grams of potatoes or other seasonal vegetables, flour (on occasion), some jam, a little meat, soup three times a week — usually barley, oatmeal or pea — 46 grams of cheese, 175 grams of sugar and a little salt.

This was clearly not enough food to sustain very active young men mostly in their early twenties, and so the life-saver came in the form of Red Cross packages. One package per prisoner per week was delivered, only occasionally withheld by the guards as punishment. A Red Cross member would visit with the Kriegie officers occasionally to check on their treatment of prisoners, including the distribution of these packages. There were three kinds of Red Cross packages: British, American and Canadian. The contents were somewhat different for each, with the American and Canadian packages the most similar. For example, the British package came with one can of sardines, while the Yankie and Canucks packages both had a can of spam. There was powdered or condensed milk, a little meat, a can of cheese, margarine, biscuits, a four-ounce can of coffee, eight ounces of sugar, prunes or raisins, soap (two bars for the Americans and one bar each for British and Canadians — we won't make any assumptions about that). The American packages alone contained five packs of cigarettes. To a non-smoker like me, those cigarettes were the closest thing we had to hard currency. The division into British, Canadian or American Red Cross packages was somewhat random and the Kriegie military organization structure tried to level everything out but the most prized items, such as cigarettes, were always in high demand.

The Kriegies became very creative and innovative in how they used the various ingredients of these packages, along with the meager Reich rations, to create nutritious and appetizing meals. And when we arrived from

Buchenwald, we were amazed at how generous our fellow prisoners were in sharing their hoarded treasures with us. It was clear we were starving and very weak from illness and malnutrition, and the meals they drummed up for us felt like we were getting first class treatment at the finest hotels in the good old U.S. of A. As an example of creative cookery, it became common practice in all the huts that the stooges — as the cook's helpers were called — ground up the crackers from the packages into a fine powder, added the right measure of Red Cross tooth powder (which contained salt and bicarbonate of soda) and added melted chocolate to make a passable cake. Chocolate cracker cake was a favorite dessert in camp. We all took turns being stooges, and it meant a day of constant chores, from carrying water in the precious water containers to heat over the hut's single cook stove, to brewing the Nescafe instant coffee or tea, to washing the bowls and spoons after meals.

Life rather quickly settled into new routines — routines that were filled with drudgery, boredom and often tension between the men, tightly packed and in circumstances they did not enjoy or appreciate. For me, and I'm guessing for most of us who came from Buchenwald, the drudgery and discomforts of camp life were always seen from the perspective of our days in the concentration camp. The difference was so great and so startling to us that as challenging as the circumstances in POW camp were, they always seemed so much more manageable, compared to the life in Buchenwald.

Morning and evening appells defined our day. A bugle would sound for appell and I, being the early-rising farm boy, would usually be up with this first call. I was always one of the first to head to the room with the cookstove and eat a little breakfast of a thin slice of toast with a very thin layer of jam before appell. The watered-down Nescafe washed down the usually dry toast. Dry because the margarine was usually inedible. By the time the Red Cross packages got to us the margarine was usually rancid. Though we couldn't enjoy it as food, it certainly came in handy for greasing our shoes and helping waterproof them against the incessant puddles in the yard. A little later, a second bugle would sound, and the men would tumble out of their bunks, grab some coffee and toast and head for Appell Platz with toast hanging from their mouths.

After appell, and after I had started to regain some strength from the generous food allotments we were given, I headed for the perimeter of the huts to get some exercise. I would jog or walk, in part depending on how cold it was. While the exercise wasn't ordered, we all understood that we needed to be in fighting shape if the opportunity came to fight our way out of the camp or if we were forced to march in a camp evacuation. The perimeter walks also gave us opportunity to talk things over with new friends and to meet old ones like Jim Hastin, whom I saw often on these walks. There was a washhouse in the camp where one could shower. While it was supposed to supply hot water, it seldom did and it is amazing how in the deep of a Polish winter just how cold water can be without freezing. Soap was available, thanks again to the Red Cross packages, and we would shave up slivers of soap to wash our clothes. Shaving was usually done either in the washhouse with the cold water, or, if one could finagle a little warm or hot waste water from the stooge, by using the klimtins as basins, one could shave in the bunk room. Klimtins were used for all kinds of purposes, including ingeniously as part of many escape plots. "Klim" is milk spelled backwards, and klimtins were fashioned by remaking the condensed milk tins into all kinds of shapes for all kinds of purposes.

Some soup, usually made of barley, was provided by the Germans and prepared in the camp cookhouses. Like all German rations, it was controlled by the ration officer. The hut cook decided if the soup was to be eaten right away when it was delivered and still hot — usually about 10:30 in the morning — or if it would be reheated later using the very scarce fuel in the hut cookstove. Usually it was eaten after being brought by the ration officer. If the larder in the hut was "fat," in other words it had reserves from the Red Cross packages, the soup might be made more palatable with some raisins, sugar and klim (condensed or powdered milk). We were supposed to take turns being hut cooks like we took turns being stooges, but by mutual agreement those most talented in the kitchen usually ended up being cooks most of the time. It worked out fine for everyone as they enjoyed it. It filled their days and the praise and appreciation they received for their efforts provided sufficient reward — along with extra cigarettes.

Noon meals were usually fish, cheese, Rose Mill pate or sometimes just bread and tea depending on the state of the provisions at the time. The Germans punched holes in the cans or opened up the packages so they had to be used soon. It was to prevent the black-market bartering with guards, which had a corrupting influence on those who were supposed to be our enemies and oppressors. Often the cheese was so moldy that a good portion of it had to be cut away. Bread too was often moldy. As for the cabbage, it was cooked to kill the worms, which unlike in Buchenwald, did not make up a big portion of our protein allotment.

There was one cookstove for the hut so two rooms typically shared the cookstove at meal times. That meant two cooks and two stooges busy at work around the small wood stove. And it meant that the cookstove was busy from about 3 p.m. until about 7 p.m., with cooks from the individual rooms rotating in to cook the meals for their roommates. Wood for the stove was very scarce, and anything that could be found that seemed extraneous and potentially flammable was thrown in. The Germans provided "bricketts" of compressed wood as fuel, but it was far from adequate. So they also smartly provided a large stump-puller for the prisoners. This was a crane-like device that, when properly powered by about 10 sweating, strong men, could pull the pine stumps out of the ground. Stalag Luft III was constructed in a pine forest, and the land was cleared for the buildings and open areas. A few scattered pines still stood in the camp, but there were a number of stumps, which were yanked out of the ground with this device and dragged to the doorways of the huts for use as fuel.

The evening meals featured some form of meat, usually spam or corned beef, thinly and carefully sliced to avoid complaints from the continually hungry men. Potatoes and cabbage or kohlrabi added to the meal, which was usually topped off with some fancy dessert of the cook's design using ground crackers, tooth powder, sugar and a little chocolate.

The times in between these meals were spent pretty much as each person wished. There were endless card games — now with real cards instead of the homemade ones we used in Buchenwald. There was a theatre, which was a popular activity for many of the men who were involved in acting, designing the sets and mounting the production. There were musical bands and lots of sports activities. By the time we arrived in October, it was too cold for baseball and basketball, but a little football was played along with a lot of hockey. Ice skates had been provided by the Swedish government and the fire pool was flooded to make a rink. The skates had been confiscated for a while before I arrived because the Kriegies had found them useful in fashioning wire cutters and saw blades, but the Germans had been persuaded to return them and the games were going strong when I was there. Teams were organized — often between bombers and fighters — and tournaments were held with results posted in the camp newsroom. It might have been the Superbowl for all the excitement generated by these events.

I tended to gravitate mostly to the library. We were very fortunate by the time I got to camp to have a remarkably well-stocked library. Books of all types could be found there, and many of us spent our time studying college-level subjects and reading all kinds of novels and non-fiction works. The library was usually one of the warmest places in the camp, and the lounge chairs that had been fashioned from bed rails were in short supply, but there were tables with benches usually available. It was a warm, convivial place where quiet was usually maintained, unlike the often rowdy, noisy gatherings in the huts or outside when it wasn't too cold.

We were allowed to write letters home once a week, and I usually wrote mine in the library. The restrictions were many. One piece of paper folded in the middle was all that was allowed. And, of course, we were not allowed to comment on much of anything. All letters were read by censors, and there was not much point in sending a letter that had almost everything cut out of it. So I wrote the standard stuff, that I was doing great, missing them a lot, hungry but otherwise well, in good spirits, looking forward to coming home, asking about my sisters and brother and how everyone back home was doing. My letters finally made it home and after the relief of finding out on Thanksgiving Day, 1944, by telegram that I was alive and in a POW camp, I'm sure they provided some comfort to mother and my whole family. But I never received a letter once during my captivity. It was a matter of timing. By the time any letters might have caught up to me, I had moved on.

One other activity helped fill my time. I was given orders or instructions by the group organized by POW leaders. My job was simple. I was to hang around near the main gate and Luftwaffe administrative building for the North camp to keep a look out for guards or "ferrets" entering the camp. Ferrets were the German-English-speaking guards, out of uniform and in clothing similar to our own, sent in to listen in on conversations to detect escape attempts, bribery and other questionable activities we might be engaged in. My instructions were simple. If a German came into our camp, I was to nonchalantly give a signal to another kriege further in the camp, and the signal would be passed down to whoever needed to know it so whatever activity was going on could quickly be hidden and remain undetected. I was fairly new to the camp, and that is probably why I was sent to cover the main gate area. The further you were away from where the activities were going on, the less likely you were to know what it was. Security, even among the inmates, was tight. This made even more sense to me when I later found out, after leaving the camp, that it was my own barracks hut that was the scene of the activity. And what was the activity? Nothing other than building another tunnel from the very same barracks that the famous "Great Escape" tunnel had originated. The kriegie planners had no doubt determined that the Germans would assume lightning doesn't strike twice in the same spot, and so Block 104 would be the least likely spot for another mass escape attempt. If this had been discovered, or if another attempt had been made, I hate to think of what the consequences might have been for me. But this activity, unknown in detail to me at the time, certainly demonstrated that Hitler's attempt to break our spirit and make the Allied flyers think twice about escaping by murdering our fellow prisoners proved hopelessly naïve. We were fighters, one and all, and would be as long as we were given the air to breathe and the strength to carry on. I was proud later of my exceedingly small contribution to the continuing effort.

Our day ended with the late afternoon or evening appell. We ate our evening meal after the last appell in our room with the cook shuttling between the room with the cookstove and our room. The six of us ate our small dinner of diced kohlrabi, mashed potatoes and thin slice of spam eagerly, then waited for the treat of cracker cake or some other dessert concoction. A little coffee by 10:30, then lights out with the blackout shutters covering the windows. Another day in Stalag Luft III was concluded, and one day soon melted into the next until nearly three months went by.

13 A FIGHTER AMONG FIGHTERS

My combat career as a fighter pilot began on April 25, 1944. It ended with a very short parachute ride and a fiery crash on August 13, less than five months after it began. I had survived 43 missions, many of them the most dangerous kind of flying mission — low level strafing and bombing attacks on key enemy positions. But I had not survived my 44th. Now I was in the company of other fighter pilots and other airmen in the prison camp east of Berlin. At last I had the time, and better, the ease of mind to think back on those incredible five months of my life. There are few pleasures in life greater than sharing terrifying and life-changing moments with the very few people on earth who have survived the same kind of experiences and find the same kind of meaning and thrill in them. This special bond can be discovered not just in a prison camp deep in enemy territory, as I certainly found in those first days in camp, but even many years later. This I would find out, one day in the early 1990s.

It was an early morning in mid-May, 1944, that a waist gunner by the name of Earl Thomas climbed through the tiny hatch underneath his B-17 bomber. Earl, a Native American from a Northwest Coastal Tribe, was a big man and didn't fit into the confined quarters of the nose and tail gun positions. The waist gunner position was a tight fit for him too. It was going to be another long flight. Another in a long string of daylight raids over Berlin. Anti-aircraft fire — flak — was intense over strategic targets, and as the Allied raids intensified deep into Germany, so did the flak. German fighter planes were also a constant menace, and few bombing missions were completed without the loss of more valuable bombers and their much more valuable crews. Earl had already survived many missions, and as he climbed into his position behind the twin fifty-caliber machine guns and felt the heavy bomber roll clumsily down the grass field, he wondered whether this would be the mission that would end his flying days and possibly his life.

The bombing mission itself would be protected against the German fighters by three different groups of American fighter escorts. One group, either the shorter-range P-47 Thunderbolts or P-38 Lightnings, would escort the bombers during the first leg over western Europe on the way out to the target. The second group, likely P-51 Mustangs with their longer range, would pick them up over their target. The last group, again shorter-range fighters, would pick up the bombers as they approached the North Sea over northwest Germany and escort them back through the English channel and back to base.

On the 11th of May, our squadron was on the second bomber escort mission of the day, and I was flying in this one. We were escorting heavy bombers to Clervaux, France, when the bombers came under attack by ME 109s. It was a hit and run mission, a flash attack from on high by about eight enemy fighters. One bomber went down in flames, and one enemy fighter dropped down, smoking from return fire from one of the "Flying Fortresses." By the time our group was in a position to engage them, they were gone and we were flying back to base protecting the remaining bombers.

Two days later I was up early for the mission briefing of the day. The next day's missions were posted on a board in the operations building — a low brick building near the grass strip and parking revetments of our P-38s. This would be one of those long escort missions. Our cockpits were small, confined spaces, made smaller and less comfortable with all our combat flying gear. We literally had to sit on an inflatable rubber dinghy, which was much harder than it sounds. Add to that our bulky parachutes, then the heavy flying overalls, leather A-2 jackets, leather helmets, oxygen mask and everything else that filled up the tiny space. The cold was fierce at 25,000 feet, and the unheated cockpits were a source of misery for a lot of P-38 pilots. Our heavy leather flying coats and helmets could not adequately protect us against temperatures often 30 degrees below zero and sometimes up to 75 degrees below zero. Even with the heavy wool-lined boots and pants that we used for the long escort missions, it was still hard to keep from freezing.

But sitting on those hard dinghies in such confined quarters for hours and hours was the worst of it for a lot of us. One of the duties of the medical crews back at base was to help pilots deal with the "angry anal apertures," as the squadron's diary colorfully described the problem. Long escort missions were the worst for these problems, as well as the strange mixture of long hours of adrenalin-filled boredom as we continually scanned for the sudden appearance of our enemy.

Our mission that day was to meet up with a group of B-17s returning from a daylight raid over Berlin. We were to pick them up east of Denmark over the Baltic Sea, then escort them back to England. Bombers that had been hit over the target or on the way back and who were slowed down by loss of an engine or engines were particularly vulnerable to fighter attack. The Luftwaffe, with its flying resources stretched by strategic bombing of factories and oil refineries as well as repeated engagement with a rapidly expanding Allied fighter force, were saving their attacks for the easiest targets — those crippled bombers with the crews trying desperately to reach home one more time. It was 800 miles to our rendezvous area, much of it over water. We met up with the "friendlies" and were headed back over Denmark when we hit intense flak over the western part of that country. Flak, coming up at us from 88 millimeter German anti-aircraft batteries, brought down a great many fighters and bombers. The gunners had learned the right altitudes to set their shells for explosion and had also learned that many pilots would veer away from a close call so if one exploded to the left, the experienced gunners would shortly after place one to the right of a plane, hoping that the pilot would fly right into it. We learned to fly into close calls, not away from them — fighting our instincts all the way. Being hit by flak was partly a matter of skill on the part of the gunners, partly on the sheer volume on the angry, black puffs of exploding shells, and partly on plain old luck.

We were flying about 5000 feet above the returning bombers when the flak hit hard. It hit not only at the 20,000 foot level where the bombers were flying but it rocked those of us flying 5000 feet above them. We did what we were told to do and scattered. No sense providing a single, tight target to the gunners below. The plan was to reform once the worst of it was over and then continue on our escort mission, protecting our big brothers below us from the slashing attack of single or groups of enemy fighters.

But when the flak lightened up and I looked around, I could see none of my squadron mates. I was all alone. A powerful sense of dread filled me — not fear exactly. But a dull foreboding. This was not good, not good. I set my course back to base rubber necking all the way to keep an eye out not only for my guys, but also to protect myself against a surprise attack. The enemy would try at every opportunity, as we did, to attack from out of the sun and from above to maximize their speed as they dived down on us. I didn't like being alone out here and kept looking anxiously around while calling on the radio to try and locate my flight.

Earl Thomas was scanning the sky for enemy fighters on the return flight from Berlin. The flight path took them over the Baltic, across Denmark, over the North Sea and back to base. The flak intensity mounted quickly and once again the multiple explosions bounced the big bomber violently, as it had on so many days before. Despite the now routine nature of the attack, it never failed to cause sweat to form on the gunner's palms. Whoa, that was close, he thought. And then, one came much too close, kicking the plane wickedly and causing smoke to pour from two of the bomber's four engines. The pilot feathered the props, locking them in place. That decreased the drag caused by props spinning freely but powerlessly in the 200 mile per hour airflow. The crippled plane, far from home, over the greatest concentrations of enemy fighter bases was now very vulnerable. Worse, the escort of friendly fighters was nowhere to be seen — they had been scattered by the flak and had apparently followed the main group of bombers which, having survived the flak, were flying on full power and making top speed back to the base.

Earl knew they were in trouble. The circumstances added up to a nail-biting ride over the next few hours, circumstances that had left many of their fellow bombers hulking wrecks in the sea or smoking piles of metal on the German or Dutch countryside far below. He checked his chute, preparing for the now much more likely order to bail out.

I was scanning the sky anxiously in all directions. I didn't like being in this spot one bit. Suddenly I saw below me the familiar shape of a Flying Fortress, the B-17. My heart skipped a beat. Although I was the protector of the bomber, it felt mighty good to have a friendly to fly home with. As I quickly closed the distance between us I noticed that two engines were shot out. The plane was slow and damaged, losing altitude as the pilot worked hard to maintain both maximum altitude and maximum speed with limited power. The faster they could get home the better, but speed meant losing altitude and if they lost too much, it might mean a cold watery landing in the English channel. I tried to reach them on the radio, but that too was likely shot out as I got no response.

I now not only had a plane to fly home with, I had a purpose. Even a single P-38 flying near a crippled bomber was enough to discourage the Luftwaffe from trying to pick off the stricken plane — unless there was a whole group of them or someone young and foolish too eager for a fight. So I continued above the damaged bomber flying big figure eights in the sky. The figure eights did several things. They kept my speed up to over 300 miles per hour, which was important if I suddenly had to engage in combat. Speed and altitude are the two advantages that a fighter pilot desperately seeks in air-to-air combat. I wanted plenty of speed. The figure eights also kept me from flying past my big buddy below, which was now flying at less than 200 miles per hour. And with the sweeping motion I could constantly scan every part of the sky, including the blind spots below the long nacelle nose, and beneath the two wings. I knew through training and experience that two good eyes constantly on the alert were my best protection against sudden death from an attacking enemy.

Earl spotted a P-38 up above and behind the plane. It was doing figure eights to stay in a protective position, and the sight made him want to shout for joy and relief. With even this one fighter flying in formation, their chances of making it home were much improved. But they still had to nurse the wounded bird over hundreds of miles of enemy territory and the English Channel.

Over the channel, their altitude almost gone, it became clear to the B-17 pilot that the plane was too heavy to make it home. I watched from above as things started falling from the plane. Machine guns, ammunition, heavy flying jackets, extra equipment — anything that wasn't needed to keep the plane flying was thrown out through the open hatches. I now knew how desperate things were on-board that plane and how hard the crew was fighting to make it back. I was glad to be there. But, I couldn't stay much longer. Following the plane with the figure eights and down to the heavier air on the deck had left me with almost no fuel. I wasn't sure I could make it back to my base at Warmwell. That thought was not pleasant. Having to put down in some open field and get through an emergency landing, perhaps damaging the plane and myself, was not something I wanted to do.

"Come on boys, get 'er on home," I breathed.

The plane, relieved of extra weight, lumbered on, just above the ground. As we approached London from the north, the bird veered right. It was headed to base. I couldn't follow it to see if it made it all the way. I was running on fumes and pointed my plane toward Warmwell, southwest of London on the southern English coast. Squeaking down about 15 minutes later was an enormous relief, combined with a sweet and satisfying feeling that I had really done some good up there today.

Over 50 years later, I was enjoying a mid-summer barbeque at our church, St. Joseph Catholic in Ferndale. Fellow Catholics from some of the surrounding towns had joined us for this annual event. I sat on the end of a bench and started listening in on a conversation going on between a couple of men sitting in the middle of the bench. I recognized one of the gentlemen, a good-sized man by the name of Earl who lived on Lummi Island, a small island just across Gooseberry Point from Ferndale. I had seen him a time or two at other such church gatherings. But I didn't know he was a WWII veteran and certainly didn't know he was a fellow airman. Suddenly, I tuned in intently as Earl talked.

"We were flying back from a long mission over Berlin," explained. "We had two engines shot out by flak over Denmark, and I thought we were a goner. We were all alone, flying slow — easy target for the fighters. I was watching and waiting for them to hit us any minute," he explained.

"When was this?" I asked casually. Earl had no idea I had been a fighter pilot as I had no idea he had flown in B-17s.

"May '44," Earl said, and went on telling his story to his buddy.

"Suddenly I saw this plane up above and behind us. I thought 'oh no, here it comes,' when I noticed it had the twin tails that only belonged to one of our fighters, the P-38. I can't tell you what a welcome sight that was. That guy followed us all the way back to England, doing figure eights behind us all the time so he could stay tucked in behind us. He saved our lives, I'm sure of it."

Earl went on to explain how they had to throw almost everything overboard to lighten the ship and how they were ready to bailout if they couldn't get all the way home. Finally, I couldn't stand it any more. I stood up and extended my hand.

"Earl, I'm Joe Moser. I think I was flying that P-38."

We compared further notes, and while we can never be absolutely certain that on that day, May 13, 1944, we were comrades in arms in desperate circumstances, it is far more likely than not that it happened just as we suppose. The joy, gratitude and amazement we felt for each other that day 50 some years afterward was nothing less than if I had landed behind that bird and had discovered that one of my fellow churchmen from right near my own town had been in that plane that I was protecting all the way over Europe.

Fighter pilots have earned a reputation, probably well-deserved, for being brash, bold and brave young men who seem to not have a care in the world but who live, eat and breathe for the opportunity to go out and prove themselves by tangling with the enemy. Certainly I knew a lot of fellow pilots who fit that category perfectly. But I am not that way, and all fighter pilots are different, each with our personalities and our styles of how we fly and fight and deal with the stress and trauma of the circumstances we are in.

I was a quiet farm boy from a Swiss Catholic family. I ended up a fighter pilot because I had the dream of a great many young, adventurous boys of that time. Once I spotted a picture of the brand new P-38 Lightning, something in me clicked and deep in my gut I knew I had to fly that plane. There was no history of flying in my family and no great tradition of recklessness or risk taking. There was no great military tradition. Just dairy farmers who loved the land, family, dancing and our own unique way of life. I didn't drink and rarely smoked. Most fighter pilots — as most military men — both drank and smoked a lot in those days. My unusual abstinence turned out to my considerable advantage. Cigarettes were better than hard currency for bartering — so I traded mine in POW camp for food and other items. Not drinking was also an advantage because I was always sought out by my fellow officers to hit the pubs in the English villages near our base at Warmwell. The English villagers by this time had a well-established pattern of buying the "Yanks" in uniform a round of drinks whenever they would show up in the pub. Since I didn't drink, it meant one more for the other guys. They took turns taking advantage of my distaste for booze. And that, in part anyway, was a secret of my popularity on these trips to the villages and while on occasional leave in London or Bournemoth.

I came by this aversion quite honestly. My dad, like many of his fellow Swiss farmers, enjoyed making and drinking his own "hooch" or homemade whiskey, which they called schnapps. Sometimes they would mix it with a little orange juice to make it taste a little better, but mostly they just drank it straight. Any get together was an occasion to break out this powerful stuff, and I did not enjoy seeing what it did to my uncles, cousins and other family members and friends. Particularly, I hated what it did to my dad. My distance from him as I was growing up was due in part to this unfortunate activity and his consequent harshness to me. He also tried to get me on many occasions to overcome my resistance and share in his enjoyment.

Homebrew beer was the beverage of choice of the farmers during the hot days of haying season. At this time, we still farmed with horses, and the hay was cut and hauled to the barn as un-baled, loose hay. It would be hauled up to the haymow using a rope and pulley with forks attached to the rope that would grip a load of the loose hay. This would be pulled up by hooking the rope on the pulley to the hitch of horses and then walking them away from the barn, hoisting the load of hay. The workers in the mow would then grab the load, pull it into the mow and spread it evenly for storage. My job was to tie the rope to the horse hitch and giddy up the horses away from the barn to pull up the hay. One of our neighbors thought it would be fun to see what a bottle of the strong homemade beer did to me, then barely a teenager. I tried to swig down the bitter stuff like I was a pro, but didn't have even one bottle before it made me completely stupid to the point where I was walking the horses back and forth, toward the barn, away from the barn, without hooking the rope to the horses. My dad and neighbor and fellow workers greatly enjoyed my little stupor as I walked those horses back and forth thinking I was pulling the hay up to the mow all the time — and being a cool Swiss farmer all the while. That beer ended up making me sick and was one more reason why I just stayed away from any drink in those days.

I never drank in high school, and this carried into my military days. I have no strong moral stance against alcohol and certainly enjoy an occasional glass of wine, but the lessons I learned from its affect on me and my loved ones kept me from the all-too-common abuse I observed among my fellow flyers.

Aside from drinking and smoking too much, one common perception of fighter pilots is that they were always eager to get into a fight with the enemy and prove their stuff. It's true, a good fighter pilot, like a good athlete, has to have the confidence and eagerness of the baseball player who begs the coach to put them in the batter's box in the bottom of the ninth when the game is on the line. It is also true that our training inculcated a fighting spirit that tended to make us eager to attack the enemy and prove ourselves in the process. A great many fighter pilots exhibited these tendencies. Some of this feeling was captured by Lt. L. C. Beck in a book called "Fighter Pilot," which he wrote during the weeks of hiding out with the French Underground. Beck was caught in the same net of betrayal that caught most of the fellows with me in Fresnes and Buchenwald, and he was one of only two of the original 168 who died in Buchenwald. But his manuscript survived and contains a vivid account of this all-American, proud and eager young fighter pilot.

Beck wrote: "I often wonder just what everyone of us will do and how we'll feel when we return to our homes to a quiet, peaceful life. To kill someone doesn't really mean a thing over here, and after awhile one seems to enjoy doing it. I know that every time I turn and dive in for the kill my pulse quickens and I feel just as I imagine a real killer of the jungle feels. We all feel, of course, that it is right and that we are doing it for our country, but still I think it brings out a certain jungle instinct in us which seems to thrive on killing."

But this was not my view. I never lacked courage, but I did not have the blood lust to kill as many enemy as I could, nor the unwavering confidence that I could and would survive any one-on-one encounter with Hitler's finest. While I had many opportunities to strafe and attack targets at close hand, I did not have the occasion to attack individual soldiers or groups of them outside of their vehicles. Many of my squadron mates did, and many a young German life was ended on the roadways of France with their last image in this world being the flashes from the fifty caliber machine guns in the nose of the P-38 from the "Retail Gang."

I remember one day being disgusted by this aspect of the life I now had. Our fighter planes were assigned to us as individual pilots and so became a part of us it seemed. We were a single fighting machine — pilot and plane. But we also had to share our planes as there were more pilots than planes in a squadron — particularly when planes were being repaired. One pilot — a fairly new replacement to our unit — was assigned to my plane for an early morning mission, and on return the pilot talked about strafing endless columns of soldiers. I used the plane on a mission later that day and found out just how much shooting he had done with it. The four 50-caliber machine guns, along with the single 20-millimeter cannon, were deadly in ground attacks. Tracer bullets were dispersed throughout the belts to enable us to more easily see if our bullets were hitting our targets. But tracers were notoriously less accurate than the high explosive and incendiary bullets that filled most of the belts, and so I would watch for the hits on the ground or on my target to see if my aim was true. Our mission on that afternoon flight was to attack a rail yard, and down we went in a screaming dive. To my amazement, I couldn't see a single bullet hitting my target. As I zoomed up and leveled off, I shot my guns to watch the tracers and see where they were going. They were making huge arcs in the sky. They were never accurate, but this was ridiculous. We didn't make a second pass at the rail yards — we avoided back to back attacks on strafing targets because it took away our surprise and gave the enemy time to train whatever weapons they had on us. Even a well-placed or lucky rifle shot could take a fighter down if it hit in the right place — like between the eyes of the pilot. But we saw a truck convoy and swooped in to attack. Again, I could not see my bullets hitting at all. It was if I wasn't even shooting.

We returned to base and I asked my crew to check the guns. They taxied the plane to the gunnery range and shot the machine guns and cannon. My squadron mate had completely shot the rifling out of the gun barrels, so indeed my bullets were flying wildly as if firing a 30.06 bullet out of a shotgun. All the barrels had to be replaced. I was not happy. When he bragged about taking out columns of enemy soldiers with my plane, I now knew what he meant. That kind of carelessness with valued equipment — perhaps driven by an extreme eagerness for the kill — was not something I understood or appreciated.

My flight instructor had criticized my flying and almost washed me out of basic training for being too "mechanical." I'm not sure if this is what led me to my later career in heating and air conditioning systems, or if that career came about because I am indeed mechanically inclined. I envied those pilots who flew with a sense of freedom and abandon that is the romantic picture of the "knight in the sky." But there is something to be said about mechanical precision in flying as well. I most admired those pilots, like Captain Larson, who were technical, precise, disciplined and still very smooth. The more freeform, herky jerky flying of a pilot and leader like Major Glass frightened me and caused many unnecessary dangers in my mind. Flying in formation with Glass all day was a very tiring experience. But being mechanical did not at all mean emotionless.

That was clear on my very first flight into enemy territory. It was April 25, 1944, and we had been at our new base at Warmwell on the south coast of England since March 11. We had spent the six weeks since our arrival in increasingly rigorous training. We all knew that one day we would be called into combat and that day finally came on April 25. Captain Glass led the entire squadron of 16 planes into the air. It was a Group fighter sweep, which meant that the 428th, 429th and 430th squadrons — all of the 474th Fighter Group — would fly together. A fighter sweep meant that we would fly into enemy territory hunting for enemy fighter planes to engage. Our target area was Rennes, France, south and east of the Normandy coast. While it was tremendously satisfying to me and to all the others to finally get into actual combat flying, our nerves were completely on edge.

"Bandit, three o'clock!" one pilot called shortly after we had crossed the channel into enemy territory. His voice was higher pitched than we had ever heard him before. We all had sworn we would not be able to turn our heads to look around, we were so encumbered with clothes, helmets, parachutes and dinghies, but the instant we heard the call of "bandit!" we were all swiveling our necks like nothing was constraining us. It was see first or die first, and we were intent on not dying — at least not on our first combat flight.

"Bandit, 10 o'clock high!" another frightened rookie called out. The entire two-and-a-half-hour flight was punctuated by frightened calls of potential enemy aircraft, but the only ones that appeared were the ones in the adrenalin-fed imaginations of the inexperienced pilots. We all returned to base, exhilarated, exhausted and, to at least some who called "wolf" a little too eagerly, also embarrassed. But, we were no longer combat virgins. We had gone out looking for the enemy, ready to engage, ready to put our training, fighters and lives on the line, and we had come back. According to our squadron diary, written by our S2 or Intelligence Officer, Karl

Swindt, the pilot's room where we gathered after a mission was a noisy place that day. For 15 minutes everyone talked at once, while Doc Carl rationed out two ounces of whiskey to those pilots who wanted it. The place sounded and looked like a turkey pen at feeding time. Finally, from a few, we managed to get a report on the mission: "fair weather, good flying, no enemy planes seen, no shots fired."

I was, I knew, at last a real live fighter pilot. Confident, but not cocky. But as ready as I could ever be for the life and death challenges ahead. They would come soon.

14 A ROOKIE NO MORE

When all come home after a mission over enemy territory, the high spirits of the young men abound. So it was on the return from that first combat mission. But it would not be long before the reality of the dangerous game we had been brought into began to hit us. On May 7, we were assigned two missions for the day. The first was to escort B-26 bombers over France; the second, the one I was assigned to, was a fighter sweep over Reims. Captain Glass — now Major Glass after his promotion on the 30th of April — led both missions. On the escort mission, a group of 15 or more German Focke-Wulf 190s jumped the formation from out of the sun and from above. Lt. Buford "Hugh" Thacker was last seen going down with his left engine on fire. He disappeared into a cloud bank, and no one saw a parachute. Lt. Milton Merkle was a recent addition to our squadron and joined us on April 23, along with Bob Milliken. Milliken would become the 429th's only combat ace with five enemy planes shot down. Merkle was hit at 10,000 feet by one of the 190s while flying in Colonel Wasem's flight. The Colonel believed he saw Milton falling away from the plane, but because of all the activity of the fighting and the cloud banks he could not be certain he saw a parachute. Losing two of our guys, especially Thacker who had been with us all along and who was a popular and lively fellow, was a bitter reminder that we were engaged in a very serious business. Of course, many more reminders of this were to come.

As it turned out, Lt. Thacker walked back into our base at Warmwell on June 16, a little more than a month after he bailed out. His face was scarred from the burns he received from his dying plane, but the French underground had hid him, helped him dress as a French peasant and provided a guide to help him get over the steep, rough mountains that separated France from Spain. From there he made his way back to England and Warmwell. Merkle was not so fortunate and became the first fatality of our squadron.

While we took our licks, it was on this mission that we got our first licks in as well. Lt. Herman Lane was flying wingman for Colonel Darling, and a

190 got onto the Colonel's tail. Just as a good wingman is supposed to do, Lane got on the 190's tail and pounded him. He fired 104 20-mm cannon shells and 907 50-caliber bullets at the enemy fighter, observing just before the fighter disappeared into the clouds that hits were appearing on the wing roots of the enemy. He claimed it as "Damaged" back at the briefing, but when the gun camera film was viewed, his claim was upgraded to "Probable." And that was worth a celebration.

I flew on that second mission in a fighter sweep, but all we ran into was flak. I say all we ran into because flak brought down more planes than anything else, but it's hard to feel heroic about surviving those dirty, rough bursts. We returned at 9:30 that night, exhausted but safe.

It didn't take too long to change from high-strung combat rookies to experienced, professional fighter pilots. It is true that the thrill of sliding those throttles forward and feeling all fourteen hundred and fifty of those horses contained in the twin Allison 12 cylinder engines pulling me into the deep blue never diminished. But neither did the gut-chilling dread of knowing each time we left the "comfort" of our cold, drizzly southern English base, it might be our last time. Last time to feel the rush of power, last time to enjoy the camaraderie of fellow pilots, last time to write a letter home. The month of May, 1944, ended with three officers lost — Thacker, Knox and Merkle. Our unit now was fully loaded with a total of 324 men, including 50 officers and 274 enlisted men. I was very proud that I was one of 18 officers in our squadron to receive my first combat medal, the Air Medal, for my work during this month — my first full month of work as a fighter pilot.

In late May and early June, ground attacks switched into high gear. The Ninth Air Force was assigned to primarily support the ground troops in tactical bombing and fighter missions, unlike the Eighth Air Force, which was more focused on strategic bombing. We were sent on mission after mission to attack railroad marshalling yards, other transportation facilities, bridges, truck convoys, trains and just about anything else that looked like it might hinder a successful invasion. We all knew it was coming. We were located on the southern end of the English island, and it seemed like every able-bodied soldier that the Allies had was headed for southern England. All of our outgoing mail was blocked.

On June 2, 1944, Captain Larson was the flight leader for a mission with pilots from our Group that was to attack a key bridge near Bennecourt. This bridge crossed the Seine river west of Paris, and, in retrospect, it is easy to see that cutting off this bridge would hinder German reinforcements being sent to Normandy. This was a true dive-bomb mission where our training in dropping bombs on pinpoint targets would be critical. Captain Larson led the mission with Lt. Al Mills as his wingman. Banks flew lead for the second wave, and I was his wingman. We sensed now that we were participating in a military operation like nothing the world had ever seen. So when we studied the maps in the briefing prior it was with a fierce sense of purpose. While we also carried maps in one of the big pockets in our flying pants above our right knee, we tried hard to memorize every little detail of our target. The bend of the river, the railroad track approaches to the bridge, the layout of the nearby town. If we did our jobs, success might mean many saved lives for our boys who had to get into the water and onto those beaches — though we did not know when or where as yet.

Our fighters were loaded down with the heaviest ordnance they could carry — a 1000-pound high explosive bomb under each wing. The load could be felt as we lifted off into the clear air. There was no sign at this time of the late spring storm that would delay the launch of Operation Overlord for a day and cause misery for our troops. We climbed to 8000 feet and could make out the landmarks below us from the briefing map. Captain Larson led us to the target unerringly and called it out below. Dive bombing was dangerous business. We had to release our bombs at about 1500 feet as we pulled out of a dive at over 400 miles per hour. If we didn't time it just right, we would be caught in the bomb blast of the plane ahead of us — and that could be deadly. In fact one of my friends, Clarence Moore, was killed on July 14 during a mission I was on while we attacked a railroad yard with delayed-fuse bombs. His plane was sent out of control by the blast of the bomb that was released by the fighter ahead of him, and we watched his plane do a complete roll before spinning into the ground and directly into a stone building. He had no time to bailout.

Adrenalin was doing its intended business as I watched Captain Larson half roll his Lightning over and begin the dive toward the target. His wingman, Al Mills, followed at enough distance to make sure the bomb from the lead plane exploded before he got there. Then I turned and pushed on the control half-wheel and watched the ground fill the windshield in front of me. I had practiced dive bombing numerous times in training, but this time it was for real. I had to concentrate on the target. Forget about the planes ahead of me and the bomb blasts that would rock me as I approached. And forget about the concentrated anti-aircraft fire that was now filling the air all around my plane. I vaguely saw the tracers screaming up at me, but I kept my eyes fixed on the bridge below, now keeping it as firmly as my flying skills would allow in the middle of my gunsight. Ease it down just a bit, push that nose down. The target must be low in the sights. My bird was shuddering now as it approached the top speed of over 400 miles per hour. Thoughts flew back quickly to my near-fatal dive experience while in training when I experienced the compression problem of the P-38 and barely managed to pull out of a steep dive. I was now going in at about 20 degrees and was approaching the release altitude. A blast came up from the water below, but I kept my eye fixed on the target, not caring whether or not the Captain or Mills had hit the bridge. I was determined to hit that thing or die in the attempt. My teeth were clenched tight with determination.

Dive bombing is simple in concept but takes skill to execute. You don't just drop the bomb at the target. You use the momentum of your diving fighter to fling it at your target. To do that, the target has to be kept low in the gunsight. Then, as you hit the release altitude, there is one brief moment when the target is dead square in the middle of the crosshairs. That's when you push the bomb release button on the control wheel.

The explosions and flak were jerking me around, but I kept the target as tight underneath the horizontal crosshair as I could. My right hand was on the control wheel, and at 1500 feet I eased off the heavy pressure I had been keeping on it to keep the plane in its dive. Now as its nose began to lift I watched the bridge pass through the center of my target. I pushed hard on the bomb release, and the plane felt like it had hit the bottom of a bungee-cord drop with the release of all that weight. My high-speed dive converted into lift as the 2000-pound weight dragging the fighter down dropped off, and I zoomed into the blue sky. Then I noticed just how thick the flak was all about me. This was a heavily defended target. I looked back as I flew up, and while the bridge was there as a target when I was in my dive, when I looked back, it was gone. Mine were not the only bombs that took it out. But I had the deep satisfaction, and still do, that I had hit the target square and done some real good that day. Our squadron finished the attack by going after the second span and then by strafing the railroad tracks that were busy with traffic on the eastern bank. We then returned to base.

It was the most successful early dive-bombing mission of the entire Group. A photo of our handiwork, with the first span of the bridge completely knocked out, is included in our squadron history, compiled by our intelligence officer, Karl Swindt. It is the only such photo of bomb damage from our squadron in this book. A lot of celebrating went on that night. It so happened that a long-scheduled Group Officer's party was held that night and the entire Group was in high spirits over this achievement. I was very proud to have been selected by Captain Larson for this attack and to have been a major contributor to its success. My flight instructor might have considered my flying style to be too mechanical, but the precision approach proved valuable on this and many other successful missions. This success, along with the other successful missions, resulted in my promotion to First Lieutenant on July 10, as well as to my being awarded the Distinguished Flying Cross. This medal, one of the highest the Army Air Force has to offer, was announced in our squadron history as having been issued to me on June 22, 1944, under Ninth Air Force General Orders No. 109. Unfortunately, I never knew about it, as I was in German hands by the time the higher-ups came around looking for me, and in the process of being released from military service, this little detail never quite caught up with me.

On June 5, at 4:30 in the afternoon, all of the officers of the entire Group consisting of Fighter Squadrons 428th, 429th and 430th — about 150 of us — were called into the Officer's Club for the most important mission briefing of the war. On maps that were hung all over the walls was described the greatest and most meticulously planned military operation in history. After a thorough briefing by our First Army Liaison Officer, Major Mulholland, we were given our radio call signs, and then someone read a message from General Eisenhower, the Supreme Commander of Allied Forces:

> *"Soldiers, sailors and airmen of the Allied Expeditionary Force! You are about to embark on the Great Crusade, toward which we have*

*striven these many months. The eyes of the world are upon you. The
hopes and prayers of liberty-loving people everywhere march with you
… I have full confidence in your courage, devotion to duty and skill
in battle. We will accept nothing less than full Victory. Good luck!
And let us all beseech the blessing of Almighty God upon this great
and noble undertaking."*

Then our Chaplain, Leon Milner, stood up and offered a simple prayer:
"Give us strength, courage, guidance and understanding in the days to
come, and protect us and our fellow men."

I remember the special excitement of this day that we knew was coming,
and we believed would provide the beginning of the end of this long, bloody
war. But in many other ways, it was just one more mission, more of the
same. It was more significant for the higher-ups, who had to plan and sweat
out the results. But for us, all we knew was that we had to climb into our
airplanes every day, sometimes twice a day, cross the channel, do our duty as
best we could and then hope for luck or the grace of God to get home so we
could do the same the next day. It is more in retrospect and with watching
more time and life pass by that I feel a surge of pride and gratitude to have
been there to observe and even play a small part in the greatest invasion in
history — the starting point of returning freedom to an entire continent of
grateful people.

Our squadron patrolled over the invasion fleet in the waters of the south of
England on that night, but it was dark and cloudy, and our pilots had no
sense of the vastness of the effort at that time. When they landed at about
11:00 p.m., the sky was filled with airplanes heading across the Channel. It
was the C-47s, the transport planes carrying the paratroopers over. When
daylight came, the C-47s were coming back and many landed at Warmwell
due to damage or low fuel. I recall that the first one came in on rough
engines and with the end of one wing hanging down like the broken wing
of a bird. The co-pilot and flight engineer stepped out of the plane to greet
the ambulance crew. The pilot was dead. On the first pass over the target all
the paratroopers had gotten out except one. The pilot circled the landing
zone again so the last trooper could jump, but as he circled a small-arms
bullet hit the plane, killing the pilot almost instantly. The paratrooper got
out and the co-pilot brought the plane back. It is quite possible that our

little base received the very first casualty from the invasion. Soon, our little strip was filled with broken men and machines, with cranes and ambulances busy hauling them off the runways so more could land or crash.

On June 8, I was on a mission to bomb railway tracks and installations in the Avranches area near the invasion beaches. We spotted three Focke-Wulfe 190s flying close to the ground, but we were low on fuel after the bombing and so returned to base without closing in to attack them. This excitement turned out to be the only time I saw enemy fighters in the air.

Ten days after the invasion, on June 16, we were into a routine of mostly strafing and dive-bombing missions, with an occasional longer bomber-escort mission thrown in. We were all thrilled to have Hugh Thacker walk into camp and give us the encouragement that it was possible to escape back to England after being shot down over France. More than that, he gave us hope for the others we had lost whose fates were still unknown. On June 21, we were given notice that there was going to be another award ceremony following a parade in front of General Kincaid, who would hand out the medals. One of those was to go to Captain Larson, who we all felt deserved that 14th cluster to his air medal for his character and leadership as our operations leader. I especially felt that way since he was my flight leader on "F" Flight. This group consisted of Captain Merle Larson, Bill Banks as Assistant Flight Leader, Al Mills, me, Bob Milliken, Joe Skiles and Dennis Chamberlain. Only three of our little group would escape death or being shot down — and I was not one of the three. Bob Milliken would become the only ace of the entire 429th.

The parade was almost over when we got the word that a mission was on. The award ceremony would have to wait. Unfortunately for Captain Larson, it would have to wait a long time. He led the squadron on a low-level attack on an enemy airfield about 10 miles northwest of Dreux. His plane was hit by flak and caught fire. Banks, his wingman, watched his chute open and circled over him to make sure he landed safely, then waited until he got out of his chute and headed for nearby woods. I wasn't on the mission but was devastated when I heard the news. Captain Larson was my flight leader, my mentor and probably the best officer in our unit — and the best pilot. Somehow, if a crafty, careful and veteran fighter pilot like he could get it, any of us could. We were in a very dangerous game, and I think I felt more vulnerable at that time than any other. Still, we all expressed confidence that, like Thacker, he'd return to us before long. Larson had already been shot down once, over North Africa, and had walked through enemy lines to safety. If anybody could make it out, certainly he could. But, of course, he didn't. In less than two months we would meet in Fresnes prison and share the rest of the war as "guests" of the German war machine.

The Allied forces were bogged down in Normandy. The expected breakout to begin the march toward Berlin and to end the war before Christmas just wasn't happening. We flew mission after mission, mostly to interrupt German reinforcements, sometimes to serve as bomber escorts, and sometimes — as on June 25 — to fly a protective patrol over a gaggle of warships, including the battleships Arkansas and Texas, which were pounding the port of Cherbourg. Even though our boys were bogged down in the hedgerows of Normandy, our contribution as fighter-bombers was greater than anticipated. General Omar Bradley, writing on June 20 to Major General E. R. Quesada, the Army general who had responsibility over the Ninth Air Force, wrote: "Their ability to disrupt the enemy's communications, supply and movement of troops has been a vital factor in our rapid progress in expanding our beachhead."

June ended with the loss of Merle Larson and Lt. Paul Heuerman, who went down on the 29th. June also ended with many briefings about packing our belongings and shipping over to France, which was exciting. Though this was what we all wanted, Warmwell had become home, and although its comforts were scarce, we knew that a forward airfield just behind the lines would not live up to the standards we enjoyed in England. Besides, would the French be as generous with their boozy salutes to the "Yanks?"

The first two days of July were soggy and rainy — impossible for low-level missions. On the third of July I was given a seven-day leave. I don't recall how many missions I had in, but it was well past the 25 that earlier in the war was considered a tour of duty. I had completed at least 30, and the intensity since the invasion was great. I was still hurting from the loss of Captain Larson, so I welcomed the chance to go to Bournemouth.

Bournemouth, resort town. Few miles from Warmwell. Beautiful weather.

In a hotel. Compared to earlier passes, this one was pretty quiet. Larson's loss affected me more than any other of the now frequent losses. He was such a good pilot. He always knew where he was and had great situational awareness. Other flight leaders were much harder to fly with — you would be worn out by the time you were done. They would change speeds all the time and would fly with herky jerky motions and sudden, unexpected disruptions. Larson was very smooth, easy to follow and easy to fly with. I felt fearful and vulnerable that he was gone, and while I tried not to let it show, it must have. Officers chose who would be selected for the seven-day pass in part on how many missions they had flown and in part on the assessment of senior officers as to who needed rest.

The seven-day leave would be the first and last for me. Most of our leaves had been 48-hour passes. Every month our outfit would have a dance, and someone would go into town to pick up the girls who wanted to go to the dance. They would load the girls up in the back of a two ton truck and haul them to the dance. One night Banks, Mills, Larson and I had a late mission and by the time we got our planes down the dance was already underway.

I wasn't much of a dancer and also was pretty shy around the young ladies. So I was what would now be called the designated driver. At midnight the trucks arrived to take the girls back to Bournemoth. Banks, Mills and Larson by now had each found a girl to escort back home in the truck. I kept trying to get the guys and girls in the truck. I'd get Larson with his girl in the front seat and then try to get Banks and Mills with their girls in the back of the truck. By the time I got Banks and Mills in the back, Larson and his girl would jump out of the front and go into the party and get another drink. I'd get them back in and then Banks and Mills with their girls would be gone. By the time I got them all in, the truck was moving and pulling out.

Since we had a 48-hour pass, we were going to drop the girls off and then stay in a hotel in Bournemouth. When I tried to get Mills out of the back of the truck, he sat on the tailgate and threw up. He couldn't help the girls off the high tailgate, so I had to help them get down. We finally got the girls back and headed to the hotel. Mills went in first and a minute later came running back out through the big revolving doors. He had thrown up all over the deep pile carpet in the lobby.

Finally, I got my three inebriated buddies to their rooms. As I stood at the door shoving Banks through, he said, "Joe, I think I made a date with a girl tomorrow morning. Wake me up early."

"What does she look like?" I asked.

"I have no idea. I don't know how I will spot her."

"Well, you better go to where you said you would meet her and see what turns up." I advised.

He did the next morning, but a little while later he was back at the hotel.

"Did you find her?" I asked.

"Yep," he said.

"Why aren't you on your date?"

"I saw what she looked like."

I did have one date during my stay in London. One of my flight school buddies had ended up in a bomber group and had run low on fuel after a bombing run over Berlin. Knowing they couldn't make it back home, they flew east to Russian-held territory and landed. He had just returned from Russia and had leave to London. He talked me into accepting a blind date with him. Turned out she was an opera singer. Yodeling is more my style. I never asked her out again.

The seven-day leave was different. It was quiet, peaceful and restful. But a heaviness lay on me that I could not shake. Too many missions, too many friends lost, and now Captain Larson was gone. How much longer could I last? While these days of peace and quiet were enjoyable, I could never escape the reality that very soon I would be climbing back into that cramped cockpit and facing a very dangerous and uncertain future.

Back at the base, I missed a memorable Fourth of July celebration. The men, being deep into a sodden celebration with some RAF flyers, complained to the Brits that this Fourth of July was pretty sad compared to the kind of celebrations we were used to at home. Huge fireworks displays and all that. The two RAF pilots slipped out and, taking advantage of an opportune moment, managed to gather a number of Very pistols, flare guns and shells from the control tower. They proceeded to chase each other around the field firing these bright emergency lights at each other, until one got away and entered a latrine window. The latrine happened to be occupied at the time by an RAF Wing Commander. His noisy, dropped-pants protest seemed to fan the celebration flames, and suddenly it seemed everyone had flare guns and other incendiary devices. Even the controller in the tower had joined in. So, despite blackout requirements and completely unauthorized fireworks, the base enjoyed a memorable Fourth of July. All the while, I was quietly trying to restore some peace and confidence to my troubled soul in London.

I returned from leave on July 11, feeling somewhat refreshed and mentally prepared to resume my duties. I found out I had been promoted to First Lieutenant. Now there was no longer a hint of the swagger of the rookie or the doubts and questions about how I would do in real combat. Sure, I hadn't been in a dogfight — yet. But I had faced all the dangers this line of work represented and had survived. Still, I knew my survival was not so much a matter of skill — or even luck. I had more of a sense than ever that what would be would be, that I was in the hands of One who had control over this entire mess, and those were good hands to be in. So I faced the work ahead with more of a sense of determination to see it through whatever lay ahead. But there never was a time when it was harder to climb into that cockpit and intentionally fly into deathly danger than the day after I returned from that leave.

Early on the morning of July 12, I forced myself to climb into that cockpit and headed on another attack mission in the Rennes, Angers and Laval region. We were back at base by 10:00 a.m., and nearly 100 railroad cars were smoking wrecks or severely damaged. It was July 14 when my friend and much-respected pilot, Clarence Moore, was hit by a bomb blast from the plane ahead of him and killed. It was another serious blow to me and my fellow pilots.

Clarence was a good friend but one of those who drank too hard. One night I and a couple of others were helping him to his bed in our bunkhouse after a dance. He was hardly able to walk. After we stripped all his clothes off and got him to bed, he said he needed to go to the bathroom. The latrine door was right by the main door of the bunkhouse, and after a bit someone yelled, "Clarence is gone." He had kept right on walking, stark naked, out the front door of the bunkhouse. We caught up with him just as he was opening the door to the still-lively dance. We got him put back in bed, and he stayed there. Now he was gone. A bright, happy young man in his early 20s who had expectations and hopes for life just like all of us.

On that day, our squadron reached a grand total of 75 missions completed. July 18 saw our squadron get caught up in the biggest-mass dogfight up to that time. I was not on the roster for the early morning mission. It was an epic fight, and the next day the Stars and Stripes reported the event this way: "Ninth Air Force Lightning fighter-bombers about to dive bomb a railway bridge crossing the Eure River south of Pacy-sur-Eure yesterday were attacked by over 50 FW 190s. Although outnumbered almost two to one, the Lightnings destroyed 10 of the enemy, probably destroyed another six and damaged 14 — and demolished the bridge." We were not without loss. Lt. Glenn Goodrich, from Ellensburg, Washington, was killed. His plane was damaged by an enemy fighter, and he couldn't fly it out. He had time to bail out, but his plane was heading directly for a small village. He deliberately crashed it into a field near the small village of Longnes, France, keeping the plane from hitting the populated area. Another heroic act, recognized now only by a small monument near this town.

On July 25, we participated in a mission that Ernie Pyle later wrote could be considered one of the historic pinnacles of the war. It was the closest coordination between ground troops and air forces of the war. The stalemate on the ground was frustrating the planners, and an all-out effort to break out was called for. Heavy bombers saturated an area where the ground troops were to move into, medium bombers hit hard closer to our troops, and the 474th was assigned a target area nearest the ground forces, who marked out the target area with red smoke flares. We received some small-arms fire, and although we saw this as a routine mission, this kind of close-air support was to become an increasingly important part of our focus. It contributed significantly to the much-delayed breakout out of the Normandy area.

Bill Banks, one of our most popular and experienced pilots and a Flight Leader of my flight, had become increasingly nervous as the weeks wore on. He had started with six bunkmates, and now he was alone. There was talk of his room being hoodooed. When Captain Larson did not return as we expected, Banks wondered aloud if anyone could survive if the Captain couldn't. Then, on an armed reconnaissance mission on July 27, the Group was attacked by 25 or more Bf-109s. A Lightning from the 430th flew into Bill's plane and sheared off a chunk of his wing. He struggled to keep it under control but others saw it start to spin. His parachute was seen opening before drifting into a cloud. After he failed to return, some of the pilots went to his room in the Officers Quarters and boarded up the door. The jinx was now complete.

The 28th of July I was assigned to a bomber escort mission over Chartres. Takeoff was at 6:30 p.m. Shortly after takeoff, our controllers intercepted German radio traffic that vectored their fighters to attack us near LeHavre as we formed up with the B-26s. We were warned to prepare for the attack. I thought my time had come to mix it up with the Jerries, but as we approached the anticipated battle area, our controllers relayed that the German fighters had begged off the fight saying they were low on fuel. It was just one more heart-pounding, exhausting flight.

By this time, we had received orders to pack up and move to France. The long awaited breakout was finally beginning, and we would be among the first to relocate to liberated soil. Our demonstrated ability to provide the combat troops with much-needed close support was critical. Captain Holcomb had replaced Larson as our Assistant Squadron Leader, and he led us on a dive-bombing mission on Sunday, July 30. It was a beautiful, clear morning, and we came back having cut up the target rail lines in two places plus damaging five locomotives and freight cars. But the flak was intense and seemed an ominous warning of what was ahead.

So July ended with us packing our belongings in preparation for a move to France. The advanced echelon left for France the last day of July. We had lost four good men: Banks, Levey, Goodrich and Moore. I was now a First Lieutenant and added the Second Bronze Oak Leaf Cluster to my Air Medal. More than that, I was alive and still fighting.

Our advanced echelon of nine officers and a group of enlisted men were over in France trying to create an airbase out of a French field near Neuilly-La-Foret. The report back about conditions was: "Stray German cavalry horses are pastured along with many cows in the lush grassland around our tents, and fresh milk is delivered to our doorsteps on the hoof. As a matter of fact, the cows are so numerous we often have to drive them away to make room for our equipment. Apples and wild blackberries now augment our daily diet of K rations. All in all, the outfit looks like a wild, roaming band of gypsies, scattered around as we are in this pastoral setting." A bulldozer was busy carving a suitable landing strip out of the now dusty-dry farmland. A steel mesh landing carpet was laid down over the leveled ground. On August 7, the new strip was ready and I took off from Warmwell for the very last time.

We landed on the dusty strip, and by August 8 almost all of us were in place in our small tent city. Good news greeted us. Two of our pilots that had been lost in July, Banks and Levey, were both in Allied hands. Banks was even back in London! It was great news and again an encouragement that bailing out did not necessarily mean the end. And, of course, Banks' jinxed room was left behind at Warmwell. By now, I had become a leader of our group.

By virtue of having survived this many missions while many had been lost, plus the success I had in carrying out many of the missions assigned, the burden of leadership became mine — including Flight Leadership. I was excited but also aware of the considerable responsibility. The lives of other men were in my hands. Flight leaders before me, like Larson and Banks, had been superb pilots and men of good judgment and character. I was ready for the new responsibilities.

Our new base was not without its dangers. In addition to marauding cows, there were German mines. One of our ordnance trucks hauling a load of 500-pound bombs hit one of those mines the afternoon we arrived. Two men were killed and two critically injured. The explosion was deafening, and shrapnel ripped holes into many tents. Then, at 5:30 in the morning, the Luftwaffe gave us a little of our own medicine. We had been dropping bombs on their bases in France for a while, and they decided to return the favor. Though 30 bombs were dropped on our base, no real damage was done. Still, it was clear to most of us that dropping bombs was better than having them dropped on you, a lesson made even more clear just three weeks later in Buchenwald.

We were close enough to the front lines to hear the heavy artillery each night a few miles to the east of us. Right in the middle of the two American landing beaches, Utah and Omaha, our landing strip was less than a mile from the beach itself. The breakout from the beachhead had been a long, bloody, difficult struggle. But now, just as we settled into our new home just off the beaches, the Germans were on the run. Bombing lines — those lines on maps that indicated where it was safe to bomb without hitting our own troops — had to be changed continually as new reports came in. The pace accelerated, and the general direction was toward Paris. Our missions were now increasingly focused on the area between our base and Paris, only about 120 miles east. The breakout had focused near Falaise, and between this city and Paris, the cities of Evreux, Dreux and Chartres were the larger points of civilization. Captain Larson had bailed out about 10 miles northwest of Dreux, and now this area saw our focused attention.

While we had shot up an awful lot of bridges, rail lines and rail cars, along with assorted trucks and other transport equipment, we had not had the opportunity to go after the really juicy targets of German tanks. That changed on August 11. At 3:00 p.m. we got word that several big Tiger tanks had been spotted along a road nine miles east of Domfort. Captain "Pappy" Holcomb led the attack, and we carried 2000 pounders on each plane. The tanks had scattered and were about 100 yards apart, hiding in some trees when we spotted them. It was classic dive bombing. Thirteen planes lining up to take their turns — each trying to avoid getting caught in the bomb blast of the plane ahead. 26,000 pounds of bombs later, and the woods were shattered. Because of all the debris from the decimated trees, we couldn't see just how much damage we had done to the tanks, but we were pretty sure it had put a real hurt on them. Taking out a group of the heavy German tanks would definitely do our boys some good down there. We felt great.

On August 12, our squadron attacked an airfield near Evreux, shooting up some hangers and some Heinkel 111 bombers. Then, on August 13, I was named Flight Leader for "F" flight, and our mission was an armed reconnaissance in the Rambouillet area. What started as another routine day, still settling into our very rustic new quarters, turned into the last day of combat for me. The squadron history had this to say: "On the first mission Colonel Wasem led Ingerson, Reitz, Kirkland, Hallford, Fleming,

Moser, Clay, Glass, Chickering, and Castel. 14 trucks and 3 staff cars were destroyed. Lt. Moser's plane was hit by 20 mm flak and his right engine (sic) conked out over Houdan. Calling Retail Red Leader, he radioed he was heading for home — then he said he was going to bail out, about 12 miles north of Dreux. No one saw either the plane or a parachute, but we had high hopes that he made it down somewhere, safely."

Whiling away my time in Stalag Luft III gave me plenty of time to reflect on those days of excitement, fear and duty. Swapping stories was good therapy and an enjoyable way to spend the time with my new roommates — although it became clear after awhile that swapping stories was what new arrivals to the Kriegie world did. It tended to be frowned upon by those who had been in camp for a long time.

There was no doubt that part of me longed to climb back into the cockpit of that P-38, push on the throttles and feel all those horses propel me into the air, line up that locomotive or bridge underneath the cross hairs and push that bomb release button or squeeze the trigger with those 20-mm cannon shells and 50-mm bullets spitting out destruction ahead of me. But sitting in the increasingly frigid camp on the Polish land, I was aware that I was a lucky one. I might never be able to experience the thrill of a fighter pilot again, but I was lucky to have had those days and lucky to be alive to share what that time was like. The question was how much more of that luck — or grace — I would need before I could get back home and be with my friends and family again. Turns out, quite a bit.

15 DEATH MARCH

The BBC said it was the coldest winter in the 20th century. The clandestine radio hidden somewhere in the North compound was a lifeline of information. Sure, the Germans provided plenty of newspapers and war updates to the prisoners in Stalag Luft III, but of course those reports sugar-coated the increasingly desperate situation they found themselves in late in 1944. So we counted on the BBC to keep us informed. I had no idea where the radio was, but runners would go from barracks to barracks repeating the story as exactly as they could.

For a while there, right around Christmas, things were looking pretty bleak. From the German newspaper accounts and the BBC news, we could piece together the great progress the Russians were making in pushing the Wehrmacht out of Russia, back into Poland and toward Berlin. We could also follow pretty well the progress being made by the Allies pushing toward the Rhine river. Patton's Third Army looked unstoppable, and we figured they'd be in Berlin before Christmas, ending the war and sending us home. But, as Christmas approached, our hopes faded. Clearly something had gone wrong in the west. The BBC tried to make the best of it, but the German newspapers made it sound like they were pushing the Allies right back to the English Channel. In the meantime, the air got bitterly cold, the winds kicked up, snow became a part of our lives and the Russians kept pounding on, pushing the Germans further and further back from their defensive lines in eastern Poland.

We did our best to keep warm. The cookstove was now the most popular place in camp. Standing in rows for appell in the freezing cold with our limited winter clothing became an increasingly agonizing ordeal. Still, I thought about those we left behind in Buchenwald. The cold would be just as bitter in the dark beech forest, but wetter even. And Buchenwald prisoners had no winter clothes at all, nothing to keep them warm. Most did not have shoes. While we were hungry — always very hungry — they were starving. While we had the cookstove, even if for a short while, they were allowed no fires at all. While my bunkmates and almost everyone else in camp complained bitterly of our conditions, those of us who had escaped from Buchenwald could not share the bitterness. We knew that we were lucky. It's strange to feel lucky in such an unfortunate place, surrounded by people who are enduring the worse misery they have ever experienced in life.

As the new year came, the stories both from the BBC and the German sources once again began to change. The Allies called it The Battle of the Bulge. The Germans talked about forming new impenetrable defensive lines to keep the war-mongers out of the homeland. But we could not be completely ecstatic about the progress that now looked as if it could only end in the complete defeat of the Third Reich. The conversations in the bunkhouse and around the cookstove now centered on opinions about our fate. What would our captors do? The prevailing opinion was that they would leave us to the Russians, whom it was increasingly clear would arrive to rescue us before Patton or Monty. Some said, no, they would not want to just let us go. We were valuable as hostages and Hitler may use us to negotiate a separate end to the war with the U.S. and England so he could turn his full remaining forces to face the Russian threat from the east. Others said that with how desperate things were for the Germans, the last thing they would want to do is have to worry about keeping us around and feeding us. It took manpower to guard us, and they needed everyone who could fight on the front. We would just be taken out and shot, or better yet, they would send up a few of the Heinkels they had left and bomb the camp just as the Russians arrived.

What did I think? What would be would be. Sounds fatalistic, I suppose. But I felt that if I was to die in this seemingly endless war, why was it not in the plane crash? Or why wasn't I taken out and shot like the two who had tried to help me in France? Or like so many others held in Fresnes? Why did I survive Buchenwald? Many thousands didn't. Did they love their lives any less than I did? Did their families not count as much as mine? Was and is my life worth more than theirs? What would be would be. Perhaps I would end up as bomb dust underneath this frozen German or Polish dirt. Maybe even put in a makeshift Russian uniform and marched into battle as cannon fodder protecting the Russian troops. Or maybe I'd return home and find a quiet life with my family and friends. Maybe. What would be would be.

One possibility, which I considered reasonably likely given my exposure to German transportation methods, was they would put us on a cattle car and haul us to another camp away from danger. If they couldn't rustle up the cars, they might just march us. March us en masse in this freezing, snowy, bitter winter. Others thought the same so we prepared as best we could. We tried to make the best of the ice and cold by playing hockey during the day. Hockey wasn't my game — just couldn't quite get the hang of the ankle thing, but I enjoyed rooting for my team. But at night we began to prepare for a move. I knew we needed to take as much food as we could with us because my experience with the German passenger rail system was that the dining car was not accessible to those packed into cattle cars. My roommates and I started working on how we would survive a long march or cattle-car ride in this bitter cold. We had already done all we could to make our clothes and blankets warm, including sewing blankets together to make sleeping bags and using newspapers for extra insulation. Unfortunately, these measures wouldn't do us a lot of good on a freezing march in sub-zero weather.

I was most worried about lack of food. I had regained perhaps 15 pounds of the 50 I had lost. But I had not fully recovered my strength, and I knew too painfully well what the lack of energy from starvation can do to you. I also knew it would be that much worse while completely exposed to the elements and dead tired from long marching. We decided to build a little sled so we could carry plenty of food. Of course, we also had to save up the food, which we did by rationing as much as we could without losing strength. We used some slats from the bed to build a frame and make the runners. We used some old raggedy clothes to cover over the small boxes and tins of food we would drag.

The Germans told us nothing of their plans, so the rumors mounted. On January 27 we knew things could not last much longer. We could now hear the heavy "crumph" of artillery to the east. The Russians were indeed coming. Soviet Marshall Ivan Konev's army was only 16 miles away. At his 4:30 p.m. staff meeting on January 27, the Leader of the Third Reich made a decision: the Allied officers and men held in Stalag Luft III would be moved out of the way of the advancing Soviets and placed in another camp deeper inside Germany. Further use of the prisoners as hostages or a final decision to dispose of them could be postponed. Of course, no one bothered to tell us what the dictator decided about us. When we heard the distant rolling thunder of the battle just to the east, our anxiety increased. Something would happen. Soon. We just had no idea what.

The first of the 10,000 men held in Stalag Luft III to move out were in the South Compound. Their Commanding Officer, Colonel Charles Goodrich, interrupted a kriegie production of the play, "You Can't Take It With You," by announcing loudly, "The goons have given us 30 minutes to be at the front gate. Get your stuff together and line up!" At 9 p.m. the 2000 men were ordered to line up and prepare to move out. For two hours they waited in the icy wind. They began to move out at 11:00 p.m. The West Camp followed at 12:30 a.m. North Camp, including me, was ordered out at 3:45 a.m. and East Camp at 6:00 a.m. As we left camp I looked behind and saw a fire burning through the blowing snow. It was my barracks. Block 104 was in flames.

The book, "The Longest Mission," published by the association of former prisoners of Stalag Luft III, says they burned the barracks I called home in protest of the 50 men who were murdered after trying to escape through the tunnel that started here. But I am certain it was to hide the evidence that another tunnel was being constructed from the very building that had fooled the German guards before. I'm guessing someone didn't want that tunnel discovered and those of us who were living there hunted down in our next camp, hauled out and shot.

It was bitter cold out almost every day during this late January. Stepping out of the bunk into the strong northern wind, being hit in the face by a million stinging pellets of icy snow and sucking in my breath as the frozen air torched my lung tissue caused in me a sense of dread and fear that brought my Buchenwald days quickly to mind. Oh no, I thought, here we go again. I just hope I can make it. I'm sure the same thought was on many of those dark, slumped-over figures ahead and behind me who hunkered down against the ice-filled wind. It was nearly 20 degrees below zero with a fierce wind and icy snow. It would get down to 28 degrees below zero before we would see any sign of daylight.

The first hours were the easiest. We still thought it might not be too far to our destination, wherever that might be. We were freezing, but such misery had to be temporary. It had to be, because if it was not we would die in it, and then, even then, the misery would be temporary. We had put on two layers of pants and as many pairs of socks as we could fit inside our shoes. We wore one pair of shorts and took another with us, stuffed in a pocket. That way we could change underwear when we stopped, letting the other one dry out from the sweat accumulated during the hard march. It felt great to be out of the camp. True, we were still prisoners, and German guards marched along with us, hunched over against the wind, trying to squeeze their bodies deep inside their clothes just as we were. But, it didn't feel as much like being a prisoner while walking along the narrow country roads of western Poland or eastern Germany.

My roommates and I pulled the sled behind us. Jim Hastin was in our larger group, but I wasn't with him any time during the march. We had put as much food on our makeshift sled as we could scavenge and hoard, but it wasn't very heavy. It was just clumsy, very clumsy. We took turns, two of us at a time pulling it through the rough, frozen tracks in the snow. But the snow kept coming down, and now there was at least six inches on the ground. Deeper and deeper furrows were being cut with the edges becoming as sharp and unyielding as iron in the 28 degree below temperature. Our delight with ourselves having made a passable sled and carrying with us provisions that would take us through any circumstance we thought the Germans could throw at us began to turn into questioning, then dread. The sled sapped our energy and we had so little left to spare.

Still we shuffled forward. Step by step by crunching, slipping step. At first we walked four or five abreast, talking sometimes. But the wind sucked the air out of our lungs, and we soon slid slowly into an interminable line of single-file, hunched-over, dog-tired, frozen men. Step by step by step. The line snaked for miles through the ice-encased countryside. Light came finally, creeping up slowly, but it brought no heat or comfort. I looked up a little, hoping for just a sense of warmth, but all I could see was a fuzzy gray streak of only slightly lighter clouds. A full-blown blizzard was shooting the pellets sideways, everything a dirty, gray-white with an occasional hint of a dark, lonely house or small out-buildings. Instead of cheering us, we could see more clearly the misery of those around us, see the long line of exhausted, struggling men, and the stark emptiness of the small farm hovels surrounded by dense patches of forest.

We were given a couple of 10-minute rests, and during these we would drop into the snow on the side of the road right where we were. We had to struggle to get the energy to find a piece of chocolate or a few crackers dug out from our sled, which was becoming increasingly wobbly from its rough ride through the icy path. We huddled close together and questioned whether the sled was worth the effort. It was taking precious energy, tiring us more than the cold and unending march alone. But there was no time to find another way to pack our precious food, so when the order came to "Raus!" we continued dragging it through the frozen crust behind us.

It was probably mid-way through the afternoon when I saw my first body lying in the snow. It was clear by now that some were not going to continue the march. It is probable that the Germans shot some of those who could not carry on, but others were picked up by a German horse-pulled wagon. It was not just the prisoners who found themselves exhausted of energy and spirit. The German guards, many of them older men, also suffered in the merciless cold, wind and snow. Their rifles hung across their shoulders, no longer at the ready. The disparity between prisoner and guard disappeared in these inhuman conditions. Now we were all just men forced against our will to endure conditions that would test even the strongest to the limit.

Escape was very easy under these circumstances, and the word went out from the officers that we were authorized to escape if we found the opportunity. Opportunity? There were few guards around and they looked as if they had neither the motivation nor the energy to lift their heavy rifles to point them at us. Now we were just fellow human beings struggling together to stay alive long enough to get to the next rest. A few did make the attempt but soon found there was no place to go in the empty, snow-covered landscape. They joined back up again to share the fate with the rest of us.

"The Longest Mission," a Stalag Luft III memorial publication, reported the death of one of the young officers from South Camp. It was related by British Paratroop Chaplain Murdo MacDonald: "On the second night out, Lieutenant Jenkins, an All-American football player decided to die. I heard the summons passed along the straggling line: 'Padre Mac, you're wanted.' Retracing my footsteps, I found Jenkins on his back in the snow. He insisted on giving me what remained of his scanty rations. I stayed with him until he died, closed his eyes and ran to catch up with the main column, three miles away. The summons came again and again."

A small snow-covered mound along side the road. A dirt pile, a pile of rags? No, another American, or English, or Canadian flyer. Dead? Barely alive and soon to be dead? Who knows. Once a young man, eager for adventure, full of confidence and joy of living, pushing throttles, swooping around the clouds, fearing, loving, breathing, laughing. Now a snow-covered mound, or was it just a pile of dirt? Would that be me soon? Would I just be a frozen lump to step over or around? Another snow-covered obstacle? Would someone bury me in this tiny field? Would a marker ever find its way over my rotting bones, or would a starving farm dog haul what was left of me into that dark woods over there? Would my mother and brother and sisters come some day to try and find what was left of me on this forsaken piece of earth? Would they find the spot where I finally fell, guided perhaps by a buddy who out of guilt of living told of my final moments? Would they go seeking in those woods for any scattered bones of their son and brother?

On we marched, trudged, step by painful step. My focus became narrower and narrower. One foot in front of the other. One bitter, frozen step at a time. The road meandered it seemed without purpose or design, sometimes passing through small villages of a few pitiful houses. Sometimes it would go uphill, making the effort to put one foot in front of the other an act of sheer willpower. The snow froze our brains, froze time, froze our snot and breath to our lips, and each step was an act of courage and tenacity, each hour an eternity.

All that day we kept moving, a snow-dusted line that seemed to have no beginning and no end. The sky darkened again, and the chill became more bitter. Would they march us until we all dropped? Is this their way of killing us? Finally, after dark and after marching through the first night and all that day, we came to a village and were told to find shelter. My roommates and I, still dragging the splintered sled, found an empty theatre in the village only a little larger than some we had passed. Collapsing on the floor of the theatre, I was immensely grateful to have made it this far. We had been marching almost without stopping for about 27 hours. I didn't know it then, but we had trudged and stumbled over 30 miles. What I did know was that I had little strength left. The exhaustion became a kind of pain where it seemed difficult to even have the energy to draw breath. It was cold in the empty theatre, rows of seats aimed at a tall wooden stage framed by a large arch. Entertainment? I did not have the energy to imagine what kind of song, dance or music filled the now frigid, empty building. It was out of the wind, out of the blowing snow and we were not marching, we were laying down, backs against the heavy wood covering the walls.

We dug some of the rations out of the sled and ate them without heat and with little talk. One thing we did talk about was the sled. After not much discussion, we decided that we would not drag the stupid thing one more foot. Instead, I took a ragged old shirt and fashioned it into a kind of knapsack. I would throw that over my back and carry what few tins of food I could manage in that. The others did the same, and what we couldn't carry was left for others. We knew by now that we would die of cold and exhaustion before starvation could ever catch us. And if we feared the pain of extreme hunger, we now knew that the pain in our lungs, on our feet, our frozen hands, fingers and noses would make any hunger pangs seem inconsequential. With that, we dropped into an exhausted, uneasy half-sleep.

Morning came, and while it was noticeably warmer, the snow was still blowing about and occasionally coming down in fresh showers. Guards, themselves showing signs of exhaustion, rousted us up, and the long line of hunched-over trudging men again began to snake its way through the country-side. The rest had done me good, but at the same time I felt more than ever before that my strength was nowhere near what it had been before Buchenwald. I knew I was strong and could work alongside any strong farmhand in the county. But the men walking with me had not lost a good part of their body weight, as I had in Buchenwald, and not been starved to where their bodies were robbing nutrients from vital organs and bones. Still, I thought, keep one foot in front of the other, what would be would be, keep it going, think of nothing, no plans, no hopes, just one foot in front of the other. Then one foot in front of the other.

The kilometers slowly passed by. There was no sun, just a bit of a brighter spot in the dirty gray clouds low on the southern horizon. Still, it seemed to be warming just a little. During most of the day I struggled to keep up, struggled to keep pace with my roommates. I was frustrated that it seemed to be getting harder just to put one foot in front of the other. But toward late afternoon I started feeling better. I only vaguely remember it now, just a growing warmth and with it a growing sense of well-being. Something deep inside me seemed to be saying that I was going to be OK, I was going home and it would feel so good. I could just lie down soon, and it would be OK. What started as a surprising sense of acceptance and peace slowly began turning to a kind of euphoria. The snow and cold and wind seemed to fill me with a kind of joy and anticipation. I can remember it clearly, but I remember feeling it as if I was far away and experiencing it happening to someone else. It was almost as if I was outside myself watching myself getting warmer, more peaceful and even joyful. It seemed the sky was lightening. It didn't seem so hard now. I could go on like this forever. Forever and ever.

And then everything went dark. I didn't realize it at the time, but what I was experiencing was the euphoria that usually precedes death from hypothermia and exhaustion. My body was indeed shutting down, and by some strange and perhaps Providential mechanism I was being prepared to die. I collapsed in the snow, dead to the world. If it were not for my two American roommates, my fear of being left to die along a nearly deserted Polish country road would have been realized. Even though they too were not far from collapse, with strength and self-sacrificing love that still brings tears to my eyes, they picked me up. With the little strength they had left they dragged me, a dead weight, completely unconscious, for a quarter of a mile to the next village — a smallish town called Bad Muskau. The town, a winter resort that today sits on the river that separates Germany from Poland, had a small makeshift hospital. That is where I found myself when I finally woke up.

For many years, my greatest pain and regret of those days as a young man caught in a giant struggle on a continent far from home was that my crash might have killed innocent people in that farmhouse and that my attempt to escape might have cost the lives of two young French farmers. When I discovered that neither fear was correct, I was left with one deep regret. And that is that I did not stay in touch with those two American pilots who saved my life. The depth of meaning of what they did for me, quite possibly putting their own lives at risk to save mine, becomes more clear to me as the years accumulate. Yes, I thanked them, of course I did. But now, these many years later, if they are still alive, I want them to know with all my heart that I have never forgotten their sacrifice and great gift to me.

The hospital was really just a large room filled with beds upon which lay moaning men in all kinds of agonies. Frostbite, exhaustion, intestinal illness, pneumonia — everything. But it was warm. I slept for 26 hours without waking. I have no idea if I received any food. Simply no memory. Others in my group had found shelter in various places in the town, many in a glass or tile factory in which there was plenty of heat from the still-operating furnaces. But after 30 hours or so of rest and finally getting a little warmth back in our bones, it was time to march again. The guards went through town telling the men to get their things together and start moving.

I would not stay back in the hospital. I pulled myself out of the bed and felt every bone and muscle complain as if I was 110 years old. But if my group was marching, I would march too. So we walked through the mostly quiet town, now joined more and more by German families also escaping from the Russians, who were only a few miles behind us. That day we only marched 10 miles and rested again. I say only, but 10 miles is a long walk for almost anyone. For us, half-starved, in freezing rain, wind and snow, and marching toward a very uncertain destination and destiny, there was nothing easy about it. The weather was warming but could hardly cheer us. Instead of biting, stinging snow pellets, the wind now carried with it slanted rain, soaking all our tattered clothes and keeping us wet and chilled. And still we marched.

We marched three more days through the muck, rain and biting wind. But there were enough rest stops to keep us only mostly exhausted and not completely spent. Finally, we groaned our way into Spremberg, a mid-sized eastern German city over 100 kilometers, 65 miles, from Sagan. It was February 5, six days since we left Sagan. We were in Spremberg only a short time, maybe an hour, before they began loading us onto cattle cars. The memories of the five days in the jammed car from Paris to Buchenwald filled me with dread and anger. But at least it was winter now and the close quarters would help keep us warm. But I thought about the claustrophobic tunnels, the fighters strafing everything that moved, the five-gallon buckets for water and waste, and I just wanted to throw up.

They began pushing us into the cattle cars, which, as it soon became clear, had recently been carrying cattle. I shoved in toward the middle, expecting again that the Germans would keep shoving men into the cars until no amount of prodding, jabbing and yelling would make room for one more man. But only about 50 of us were jammed in our car. Compared to the Paris to Buchenwald ride, this was almost comfortable.

No food was provided as I recall, and once again the "toilet" ran over quickly. We leaned against each other, and the constant close-quarters jostling meant that real sleep or rest was impossible. The men were angry, overcrowded, desperately hungry and thirsty and completely uncertain about our fate. While I shared the frustration, I think the realization that if I were a cat I would be down to one or two lives made an impact on me. I'm not saying that the misery, pain or fear couldn't and didn't touch me, but there is only so much that can shake you to the core, and I think I had reached that point. Waking up in the hospital realizing that were it not for the love — I can call it nothing else — of two men who themselves were suffering and near the end, gave me a perspective on life and living that has never really left me. When you truly understand you owe your existence and joys to others who had no real reason to sacrifice themselves for you, it is hard not be affected or changed for good.

The cattle train with 10,000 flyers trundled slowly through the German countryside. After three days it arrived in Nuremberg. Nuremberg. Where Hitler and his brown-shirted goons celebrated their rise to power. And where, eventually, at least some of those responsible for the horrors that we and many others in the world were experiencing would meet some sort of justice.

We were marched from the train station to Stalag XIIID, which had been built on part of the Nazi Party rallying grounds. The camp had been used for many purposes before and during the war. It held very few American or English prisoners during the war, as they were instead most commonly kept deeper into German territory in places like Sagan. So most inmates were from Russia or other parts of Europe. When we entered the camp we knew we were no longer in Stalag Luft III. The filth of this camp was overwhelming, and not just because of the incessant rainy mud. The barracks were filthy and uncared for — very much unlike the neat and tidy condition of Stalag Luft III. The broom we had to clean up only had a few bristles left — barely enough to make it recognizable as a broom. The previous occupants clearly did not operate as the kriegies in SLIII, and it nauseated us to clean up the garbage, excrement, mud and broken items they left behind. I was asked if this was what Buchenwald was like. Yes, except Buchenwald was still worse I said, and I know I wasn't believed. It was indeed reminiscent of Buchenwald in toilet facilities, in cleanliness, in morale and in food. But here there was still hope. Another German train ride was over, and for today at least, we knew our fate.

16 MOOSBURG AND LIBERATION

From February 5 to April 5 of 1945, I was in Stalag XIII D in Nuremberg. From April 5 to April 15, I was marching alongside tens of thousands of other POWs away from the Allied advance to POW camp Stalag VIIA in the town of Moosburg. I was in that miserable place for two weeks until April 29 — the unforgettable day of our liberation.

The simple description of time and place tells little of that time. The weather was changing from the bitter cold of the northeastern German winter to the warm sunshine of early spring in southern Germany. But my memory of that is mostly of muck and rain with little sunshine or warmth. We were ever closer to liberation and freedom, but with each step of the enclosing Allied armies, our fears increased that ours would be one of those too common, too tragic stories in which the helpless soldier dies with freedom in sight. Somewhere, in the skies above, a fighter pilot would be the last to die in a war that was already over. Somewhere, a German would fire a rifle or send an artillery shell and kill an Allied soldier without knowing that peace was declared. Prisoners, the most helpless of all, could as easily fall victim to the liberator's eager guns as to the vicious bitterness of an enemy who knows he has lost and has no reason to spare anyone the fate about to fall on him. There is a constant tension between rising hope and increasing fear. If you've ever lived this way you will understand when I say sometimes we just wished it would be over rather than continuing to live with such anxiety, longing and uncertainty.

There were 15,000 POWs housed in the ramshackle wooden barracks of Nuremberg. The beautiful, medieval city had been severely damaged by the frequent Allied air raids, and we saw the destruction first hand as we marched from the train station into the camp. We set about doing our best to turn the stinking, filthy barracks into something livable without having any idea how long we might be there. The guards tried to discourage us from ripping broken boards and lumber from the worst of the shacks, but they provided us no fuel to keep us warm during those cold February and March nights. There were too many of us and too few of them for them to have much affect on what we were doing.

The food was what was most discouraging. I had regained some of the weight I had lost in Buchenwald, then been weakened again by the dreadful march to Spremberg. Now there was nowhere near enough food to rebuild my strength. Red Cross packages came only a couple of times in the two months we spent in Nuremberg, and we did all we could to hoard some of the treasures thinking, rightly, that we might need them to barter with the locals if we got the chance. So it was mostly a few potatoes, the teeth-cracking black bread, the phony coffee and the thin gruel they called soup. Unlike Stalag Luft III, there was no library, no mail, no newspapers — nothing that diverted us and allowed us to pass the time with some degree of normality. A radio had been smuggled by the men all the way from SLIII, and it gave us encouraging reports of Allied progress. But even those reports, as welcome as they were, caused anxiety. What would Hitler do with us next? Would he simply allow us to be liberated? Would he order the Luftwaffe to bomb the camp after the guards had left? Would the guards in the towers encircling us be ordered to shoot and the readily available machine guns be set up to mow us down while we lined up for appell?

Unlike Sagan, Nuremberg was a popular target for air raids. The rail yard, a favorite target of bombers and fighter pilots alike, was a short distance from the camp. So we endured many frightening air raids, reminding me of that dreadful hour in August when I was certain that my name had been called in that roll call up yonder. Sometimes the bombers would come in huge waves — Lancasters or Sterlings — on massive night raids. Other times, a single Mosquito would scream in before the air raid alert could be sounded and drop a single 4000-pound bomb with an ear-shattering, bone-shaking explosion. And sometimes the noon or afternoon sky would be filled with B-17s and B-24s unloading more destruction on the shattered city. By now, we were more confident of their accuracy, and so while awesome in power and noise, these frequent raids became part of the routine of life in Nuremberg.

Speculation rose again to a fever pitch when it became clear that the Allies were approaching from the north and west. We hoped and prayed that the guards would just walk away, disappear and try to escape the certain fate that awaited them. We sensed that liberation was close, tantalizingly close, but what would we have to endure yet before that glorious moment? It was dangerous to hope for too much. We talked openly of what we would do if the Germans just opened up on us to liquidate us rather than allow us to be liberated. We agreed we would run for it so they couldn't get us all, but we knew in our weakened condition we probably wouldn't be able to get far. It was deeply frustrating to think about being so vulnerable when it looked like the end was so near.

On April 5, two months after arriving, we were told to gather up our things and get ready to march. This time there wasn't the obvious rush, nor the uncertainty of how to prepare. The weather was cloudy and rainy, but not like the cold blizzard that we marched into leaving Stalag Luft III. We also didn't have the stores of food to carry since we had very little to take with us. Dripping from the rain, cold and muddy, we once again fell into line, three abreast, and walked down a narrow road leading out of Nuremberg. To where? Who knew? No one told us. But we were certain there was only one direction left to the German High Command: south.

The 15,000 of us marched through the countryside and small towns and villages. Unlike the desolate scene of the snow-blasted farmland west of Sagan, life was emerging in the early warmth of spring. The farmers and villagers were outside, working their fields and gardens, eager to talk and barter as we passed by. The cigarettes I saved for just this kind of occasion became highly valued, and the additional potatoes, pieces of meat and other treats made the march seem more like a picnic at times. The war was clearly in its final phase, and everyone was deeply weary. While unhappy with their lot and the uncertainty ahead, the townspeople we met exhibited more relief and friendliness than deep hatred or animosity.

We traveled about six to eight miles each day in what would turn out to be another nearly 70-mile march. A week into the march, I was walking past a farm when I spotted a farmer near his small, stone barn. He seemed friendly and happy, so I asked him if he had some potatoes I could trade for a few cigarettes. I could speak a little Swiss-variety German.

"The war is over," he said with a joyful smile, after accepting my offer of a trade.

"What do you mean?" I asked him in my broken German. Certainly he couldn't still be thinking his country was winning.

"Your president is dead. You have lost the war."

The Germans had won? Our president was dead? A group of us gathered around and fired questions, trying to understand what he was saying.

"President Roosevelt is dead. You cannot win now with your president dead," he tried to explain, fingering the precious cigarettes.

This was how we learned of President Roosevelt's death. It came as a heart-thumping shock, but along with that we could not help but laugh at this old German farmer who know so little about America.

"We have a vice president," I tried to explain. "He is already in charge, and the war is going on. Nothing will change."

We did not convince him. Understandably so. So many Germans had tied their fate and faith to "the Fuehrer," believing that as he lived and died so did they, that they could not conceive of the United States being able to carry on the war without their leader. It was also a reminder that so many of these simple farm folks, so reliant on their government for information and so trusting of their leadership, had little idea of the state of the world and the devastation of their country. Neither did many of them have much of an idea what their leaders had done in places like Dachau and Buchenwald, even though they were not far away.

Three days later, on April 15, we marched into Stalag VIIA near the town of Moosburg. About 30 miles northeast of Munich, this camp was built just north of town in 1939 originally to house Polish prisoners of war. It soon became the largest POW camp in Germany and housed prisoners from every major front and from every country. When we marched through the main gate, there were nearly 120,000 prisoners here already. The 15,000 more of us marching in was hardly a welcome sight to either prisoners or guards. The barracks in the main camp, where we stayed, were built to hold 10,000 prisoners, but during the war at least 40,000 or more were kept here at any given time.

There were of course no filthy barracks waiting for us here. Tents were set up wherever there was a spare place to put one. Men crowded into the tents, sleeping on top of each other, with some just sleeping outside to avoid the crowds in the tents. Everywhere there was the stench and filth and tension of over 130,000 men, tired, cranky, fearful, weak, hungry and vulnerable. The group I had left Stalag Luft III with had hung together during the marches and through the Nuremberg clean up, and now we hunkered down to endure this latest example of German hospitality.

The guards did their best to keep some form of order, but it was quite hopeless at this stage. It is remarkable given the overwhelming burdens that they actually tried to maintain their bureaucratic standards, carrying our SL III registration cards on the train and through the long marches, filing them neatly away in SS headquarters in the town of Moosburg. As mentioned earlier, it was here that my own personal POW registration card was "rescued" by a G.I. rifling through the abandoned files after liberation. Soon the effort of any sort of roll call was abandoned, and I was happy to put that part of my POW experience behind me.

But what lay ahead? Where could they move us to next? Our food supplies were getting smaller and smaller. In the two weeks spent at Moosburg we never saw a single Red Cross package, although after liberation warehouses were discovered stacked with them. What we wouldn't have done for the keys to those warehouses. Our hunger matched that experienced in Buchenwald. Now all of us felt it. It consumed us day and night with a desperation that makes you think that wood or cloth or a blade of grass might ease it. If cows could eat grass, why couldn't I? Why couldn't God have given me a rumen, too?

The latrines were overflowing. The sewage system created for 10,000 could obviously not handle 130,000 or more. And with dysentery a common malady, along with the overflowing latrines, the smell overpowered the body odor and other assorted pungent smells that filled the air. Our thoughts and idle talk was not just about the horrid conditions and when they would end. We knew this had to end soon. But there was enough German military activity, including tanks and heavy guns, that it was clear they were planning on putting up a fight.

It was that fight that really frightened me now. Each day it seemed to get closer. We could now hear the deep rumble of distant artillery fire, maybe 20 miles away. Being one of the last to get into the camp, I was near the main gate with its two 10-foot-wide double barbed wire gates. It was through here that the action would most likely come, and I would be dangerously close to the shooting. Like others concerned about friendly fire and getting caught in the middle of the impending fire fight, I dug a slit trench in the ground near the gate. At least I could get my head low this way if the shells and bullets really started to fly . . . or if the Germans tried to eliminate us at the last moment.

We could see a lot of German activity beyond the fence. Moosburg sat on the Isar River, and just east of town was a stone bridge over the river that was the main avenue of escape for the German soldiers retreating from General Patton's forces. Brigadier General Charles Karlstadt, Commanding Officer of Combat Command A of the 14th Armored Division, was ordered to rush to Moosburg and try to capture the bridge over the Isar before the Germans blew it up to cover their retreat and slow the advance. He had in his command heavy artillery guns, tanks and a lot of weapons, but only one company of infantry. The Germans had as many as 7000 troops around Moosburg, but they were armed with mortars, machine guns and panzerfausts — small, shoulder-fired anti-tank weapons similar to our bazookas. And they were looking to escape.

In the early morning hours of April 29, just after General Karlstadt awoke, a delegation from the Moosburg camp was presented to him. It consisted of an SS Major, Colonel Paul Goode of the U.S. Army and Group Captain Willetts of the Royal Air Force. The last two were, of course, prisoners. While Colonel Goode enjoyed a breakfast of bacon and eggs provided by the General's staff, the General listened to the proposal delivered by the SS Major: Declare a "neutral zone" around Moosburg and the Allied prisoners would be released unharmed. Of course, what Colonel Otto Burger, the camp commandant, was trying to do was barter for the escape of the guards and SS troops in the area by getting the Americans to delay the attack on the bridge.

General Karlstadt radioed division headquarters for instructions. General Albert Smith, Karlstadt's commander, ordered the General to attack the bridge and to "lead your troops into Moosburg." The message delivered by the SS Major was the first information that the Allies had that there were prisoners in the area. But there was to be nothing done to deter the advance on the bridge — a useable bridge over a major obstacle was critically important. The prisoners were returned to the camp and the rejection of the proposal was relayed back to Colonel Burger. We, of course, knew nothing of the bartering going on involving our lives. I doubt we would have agreed on the strategic importance of the bridge versus our lives, but such is war and the decisions made by those given responsibility.

Not long after, the attack on Moosburg began. The tanks moved forward with the single infantry column alongside. As they got to within a mile west of Moosburg, the SS troops, entrenched behind banks, opened fire. American tanks that were deployed on the west side of the Amper river blasted the Germans on the bank. But because they now knew there were POWs in the area, Karlstadt ordered that the large artillery pieces not be used. Thank God. The heavy guns would have probably taken a terrible toll on the prisoners, the battle was that close to us. They would fight the overwhelming German force with rifles and tanks.

On that morning of the 29th, at about 9:30 a.m., I could see the knoll to the west where the Americans were forming. Suddenly, we saw the tanks in action only a mile and a half from the camp. The liberators were at hand! But would we survive the liberation? The Germans were rushing around outside the gate, trying to get into position. We could tell they were putting up a real fight. The gunfire was reaching a crescendo. At first it looked like the tanks were stopped on the bank of the stream, but then they moved forward. Bullets and an occasional tank shell were now entering the camp and I ducked into my trench, hoping and praying for the best. Everywhere I could see prisoners scattering, hiding, getting behind buildings or taking whatever shelter they could.

The Americans were intent on getting to the bridge. They were outnumbered but the Germans were outgunned. The Germans fought hard, but soon they were either dead in their foxholes or running for the bridge. A lead tank saw the way open for the bridge and roared through the town at 20 miles per hour, trying to get across before it was blown. As it got part way across there was a huge explosion that shook the ground around my trench. The bridge was blown. The tank driver skillfully backed his tank up and off the destroyed bridge. But it was too late — the bridge was gone.

The fighting continued on, now in the streets of Moosburg and just outside the camp. The camp guards were very nervous, and some of them walked out of the camp toward the advancing Americans with their hands up. But SS officers suddenly appeared, shouting and waving at them. A few guards were shot in the back by their own officers, and the others were persuaded by this to continue the fight. I heard the clattering of a machine gun and saw that it was coming from the steeple of a church — the tallest building in town. The Germans in the steeple had a bird's eye view and no doubt had been directing fire as the American tanks and infantry attacked. But now, with the tanks in the town itself the Americans spotted the machine gun nest. A tank turned its big gun toward the steeple, and in an instant the steeple was gone. With that, the firing soon started to die down, and the battle for Moosburg was over.

General Karlstadt was now in town, and he grabbed a German captain to lead him to the camp. The General, along with two lieutenants and their jeep drivers, headed toward the camp. Suddenly they came upon a large group of guards — all armed. Brazenly, they roared toward them with hands on machine guns and ordered the guards to lay down their weapons. The two young officers and their three drivers promptly collected the weapons of 240 German guards. The captors had finally become the captives.

Shortly after this, a battle-scarred medium tank roared toward the main gate — and didn't stop. It tore the barbed wire gate apart and suddenly, right in front of me, not 20 yards away was a real American tank. There was a stunned moment. And then bedlam. A roar went up from the camp that rolled through the acres, down through the narrow muddy corridors, in between the shabby tents, into the ramshackle barracks — a roar of relief and joy and exhilaration that only the liberated can truly know. Liberation! The roar grew and grew — such a sound will lift your heart for the rest of your life if you once hear it. Freedom. Just a word, but something good and brave men will give their lives for in a heartbeat.

The tank was suddenly surrounded and then buried under dozens of screaming, yelling soldiers. I was yelling my head off with the rest of them, bawling my eyes out. If there were dry eyes there, I didn't see any. The war was over for us. It was unreal, it was greater than any fantasy, it was the answer to our most fervent hopes and prayers. And now it was here. I had survived.

There is a famous photo of this moment of liberation and I am in that crowd, just yards from that tank. No words can communicate the joy that can be seen on our faces as the realization dawned on us that we had survived the worst of what Hitler could throw at us and that we were safe. Not long after the tank entered, we watched the Nazi swastika flag come down from the prison administration building and the stars and stripes go up. I wept uncontrollably, and thinking about that sight still brings tears of joy to my eyes. That was the end of the war for me, the moment of victory I had dreamed of even before I climbed into my first training aircraft and had so feared I would never see. How sad it is to me and those of us who shared in these moments to see so little respect for that beautiful flag today and so little appreciation for freedom and its costs. When we saw those stars and stripes rise into the blue sky of that late April day and replace the black and red slash of Nazi hatred, it carried with it the meaning of almost all that is precious in this life — family, security and most of all freedom. Freedom to walk where you want to walk, to pursue your dreams and to be free from the constant fear of instant death by hanging or firing squad.

The 14th Armored Division had just liberated over 130,000 prisoners — the greatest number of the war. The unit was named the Liberators, and they proudly wear this title today. One of the tank crew was overjoyed to find that his son, a young air corps lieutenant, was one of the prisoners he liberated.

I was free, I was safe. But I was 6000 miles away from my family and home, in a devastated continent. Getting home would be the next and final adventure.

17 COMING HOME

"Do you have any food?" was the question most urgently asked of our liberators. In that newly liberated camp were 130,000 or more starving men. Their happiness to see the American tanks and GIs was matched by the unhappiness of their empty stomachs. Since I was near the main gate, I was one of the first to greet the small contingent of infantry as they entered the camp. The soldiers handed out their own rations. We eagerly grabbed them and scarfed them down, but those packages quickly ran out. Still, my stomach felt a little comfort and now I had the prospect of getting out of this place, I was in American hands, and for the first time could start thinking about getting home. So I considered myself among the happiest and luckiest men alive at that point.

We slept in the camp one more night. The Army guys had to figure out what to do with all of us. The enormous logistical task of getting hundreds of thousands of prisoners back home was just one of the jobs they had to do. Germany was still not defeated. The war was going on, and we didn't realize that the speed of attack of the Western Allies and the ground our troops captured would determine the post-war boundaries between freedom and the dark prison of the Communist iron curtain soon to descend on all the ground captured by the Red Army. By now it was increasingly clear to the American leaders, including brand-new president Harry Truman, that Stalin had no intention of keeping his promises about the post-war divisions that Roosevelt, Churchill and the Soviet dictator had agreed to at their Yalta conference. Whatever territory his Red Army held, he would not give it up — so the race was on.

The state of the world at that time was of little concern to me. The day after liberation we were directed out the open main gate, and I put Hitler's dreaded camps behind me once and for all. Walking through that main gate with my fellow prisoners and U.S. troops all around was like walking through a dream I had never quite dared to allow myself. Not that we went into instant luxury. I was billeted with a large group of fellow ex-kriegies in a big barn just outside of Moosburg. I slept in the haymow, and the hay smell brought me back to my days on the farm in Ferndale. It felt incredibly comfortable and comforting. Normally, if one sleeps in a barn, the main complaint is the odor from the farm animals. But I can tell you, the stench from myself and my fellow ex-prisoners overpowered any unpleasant odors from the animals that had been kept in the barn before us. We stunk to high heaven, and it became much more obvious just how filthy and disgusting we were when we moved from the camp to the barn.

Food was still our major concern. We had essentially been starving since leaving Stalag Luft III. I don't think I was down to my Buchenwald weight, but it wasn't too far behind. Fortunately, the troops had discovered in Moosburg a warehouse filled to the rafters with Red Cross packages. These were quickly distributed and even more quickly devoured. Only later did the anger come when we realized that the much vaunted German organization system had left all this food in the warehouses when nearby 130,000 men were slowly being starved to death. The cruelty and inhumanity of that still haunts me as I recall the pain of the excruciating hunger.

We stayed in that barn for a week. Now that may not seem like much in the overall scheme of things because, after all, how could we complain, we were winning the war and we were out of German hands. But young men fresh out of prison camp are a little like tigers which have been kept caged and hungry for a long time. The food brought fresh energy. Add to this the relief of being out from under the cloud of an uncertain future and instant death. Add even more the desire to do something useful in the fight that was still going on. And then, most powerfully of all, add the longing to get home and once again see family and friends that we had despaired of ever seeing again. We had to get out of there! Now! What the heck is the holdup? This Army is FUBAR! What is going on? Nobody knows anything. What a bunch of no-good clods! This is ridiculous. A barn full of some very pissed off and no longer very hungry men. We sat there for a whole week without a clue as to what was really going on, not even knowing if anyone was taking our lives and needs into consideration. The only thing we were told is to not wander off too far in case some transportation showed up for us. Of course, looking back on it now and even a little later, it sort of seems ridiculous to be so impatient and upset. But we felt we were rotting away in some God-forsaken little barn in the middle of a country we hated while everyone around us was simply going about their business.

Some guys did wander into town, which is likely how one young G.I. came across the POW records in the Gestapo office in town. As told earlier, he grabbed a handful of those and took them home with him as some kind of strange souvenir. Then, 45 years later he started reuniting those cards with their "owners," including me. Imagine my complete shock and surprise to find my Stalag Luft III camp registration card, including the gaunt picture taken the day I arrived from Buchenwald. For those doubters who would come later, that card which listed my previous destination as K.L (for Konzentration Lager or Concentration Camp) Buchenwald provided ultimate proof. It remains one of my most prized possessions and one that I hope my great-great-grandchildren treasure.

At about 2:30 in the afternoon of April 30, shortly after we were led from the camp to the barn, Adolph Hitler and his mistress, Eva Braun, shot themselves in the bunker underneath the Reichstag in Berlin. Their bodies were taken outside, doused with gasoline and cremated. The war was quickly winding down. The Soviet flag would soon fly over Berlin. On May 2, the German Army would surrender in Italy while the British, Canadian, French and American forces pushed east toward Berlin, Austria, Bavaria and the Baltic. While we were hanging out in the barn, German troops were fighting their way from the east to the west, desperately preferring to surrender to the democratic forces rather than the Red Army. Meanwhile, the fight in the Far East against Japan was far from settled. On May 3, just over five hundred miles south of my home, a Japanese bomb landed in Lakeview, Oregon, killing a mother and five children. It was one of hundreds Japan had sent on balloons hoping the winds would carry them over the Pacific and land in the U.S. It was the Japanese version of the "terror weapons" that Hitler had desperately hoped would turn the tide in Germany's favor. However, this is the only one of the balloon bombs that ever made it to U.S. soil.

There was an airport near Moosburg, and we were told that any day C-47s would be arriving to start taking us home. There was no mail coming in, no reliable news from anywhere and no way of sending mail out. From the day I was shot down I never received a single letter. It was not because none were written, but by the time the Red Cross and U.S. Army found out where I was and communicated that to my family, the mail they sent arrived too late. I left Stalag Luft III just before some long-ago written letters arrived, and I was on the march essentially since then. I finally got to read some of those letters after I got home because that's where they finally caught up with me. I was desperate by this time to talk to my family, to see if they were alright, just to reconnect and let them know that I, finally, was just fine.

About the second day of May, the C-47s started arriving in dribs and drabs. With no apparent order, other than random chance, POWs started being grabbed, loaded onto Jeeps and driven to the airport for the first part of the long ride home. It only made the rest of us crazy. A little planning and predictability would have helped our mood considerably. As it was, we didn't know if our journey would start in an hour or a month. The bitter complaining went on stronger than ever. We really didn't understand the immensity of the task of trying to get 130,000 men out of there with the urgency of the final days of the war going on. But better communication and information would have helped us an awful lot.

Finally, I happened to be in the right place at the right time.

"Load up," the young private told me.

"Yes sir!" I answered and in a minute I was on my way out.

We got to the airport, and there was that big, beautiful gooney bird. That's what we called the C-47, which in civilian life is known as the DC-3. Happy guys with big smiles were piling into the plane. It had room for 27 troops, and I'm not sure but I'm guessing there were that many and maybe a few more onboard. I had no idea where we were going, but I knew it would be west and would be to some safer and cleaner place than the barn.

We took off into the bumpy air, and soon after we were airborne a sharp pain starting growing quickly in my gum. I tried to ignore it, but it grew rapidly in intensity until it started to color all my senses. It was the worst toothache of my life, and all I could think about was getting on the ground and hunting down the first dentist I could find. That's why finding out about the end of the war was less than a completely joyful experience for me. While in the air, we were told that last night, May 7, the Germans had signed an unconditional surrender — in Rheims, at the Allied headquarters. The war was ending today! There was a celebration on that plane as the news broke that threatened to bounce us out of the air. And oh, how I wanted to join in the whooping and hollering and slaps on the back. But my tooth was killing me! There was just something terribly unfair in this timing.

I was on that plane for two hours — two long and dreadfully painful hours. By the time we landed my jaw looked a little like Senator John McCain's -- all swollen and tight. When we landed, much to our amazement, we discovered that we were in Rheims, the very place that was the focus of the entire world on the day the war ended. Again, my joy was circumvented by the urgent need to get my painful tooth to a dentist right away!

As soon as we landed, while everyone else was focused on celebrating and getting the bus to LeHavre, I was trying desperately to find a dentist. LeHavre was the port on the French coast where we would embark for the voyage home, Finally, someone told me about the base dentist and where to find him, which I did as quickly as I could. He took one look at the abscessed lower molar and said that it was coming out. I don't think he bothered with novacaine or anything else to dull the pain. It didn't matter — nothing could have hurt worse than having that thing in there. A moment and a jerk later, it was gone. Immediately I felt better. He packed my empty socket with that gauzy stuff and sent me on my way. I headed back to where we were supposed to get on the bus only to discover the bus to LeHavre had left without me. Mad? Yes, but my relief at getting rid of that tooth was so great that it didn't bother me too much.

I slept in a tent that night in Rheims and the next day caught the bus to LeHavre and to Camp Lucky Strike. This was a vast, sprawling American camp and was so much better than we had been used to. Rows and rows and rows of tents, but they were clean and in good shape. There were literally thousands if not tens of thousands of soldiers milling about ready to ship home. The impatience mixed with the anticipation and excitement of having survived and to be heading home created a kind of joyful tension. It seemed there were very few soldiers in charge of things. Probably because we were used to seeing lots of guards — here no guards were necessary — and also because most soldiers were in the field fighting the war. There was a kitchen tent with a long chow line and there was — unbelievably to me — plenty of food. Plenty of food! That's the first time I could say that since August 13, the year before. Actually, I have to go back to Warmwell to say there was plenty of food. That's a long time for an active young man. The latrines were clean — another first in nearly 10 months. And I had my first shower since Stalag Luft III. Think about that for a minute. It was May 10. I hadn't had a shower or bath or any opportunity to really wash up since January. OK, you get the picture. People actually smelled nice. The place smelled nice — well, OK at least in comparison to where we had been. We got clean clothes, we got haircuts, and if it weren't for my still very sore mouth I would say that life in Camp Lucky Strike was pretty darn good.

I looked around but could not find a single person I knew. We all shared the anticipation of going home, but I felt quite alone and lonely. Now that getting back with my family started to seem like a real possibility, I felt the distance and separation with special pain. I couldn't wait to get on the road, or on the ship as the case would be. And then I was told it would be May 19.

May 19 was my dad's birthday. Dad would have been 62 had he lived. He had died nine years earlier. Strange as it seems, I left for home on my dad's birthday and arrived in New York, finally back in the good old U.S. of A on my mom's birthday. It was a beautiful May sunshiny day when I boarded the boat at LeHavre harbor. This was a much bigger boat than I had come across on. It had been a passenger liner and had more of the comforts for civilian ocean crossings. Each cabin had two bunks, and I had my own bunk all the way over, an incredible luxury.

We were told when we boarded that we were not going directly to New York but instead to Trinidad to unload some air transport command troops who were still in the war. We understood, but it meant our crossing would be three weeks long. We would stay on board in Trinidad and wait for two days before heading to New York. Interminable, but who could complain. We were heading home.

As I boarded the ship I was troubled by one thought: seasickness. I had been dreadfully sick on the trip over, the ship rocking like a cork in rough water. I didn't want that experience again, and the news about the extra long sailing filled me with dread. But, this was a much bigger ship, the sailing was during a better time of the year and I didn't get sick at all.

I still wasn't able to meet up with any of my buddies, but I struck up a conversation with a fellow pilot by the name of Foster Perry. Turns out he was from Sedro-Woolley, Washington, another small town very similar to Ferndale and only about 25 miles away from my home. We struck up a friendship that lasted through the years, meeting up again at POW reunions until we buried him with a POW funeral in Sedro-Woolley many years later. Foster became my crossing mate, and we soon we had a favorite pastime in common: eating.

This passenger liner filled with eager, tired and underweight young men was not much like a cruise ship. It was like a cruise in one important item: food. There was more than enough for everyone, and it was available night and day. When I tell you what happens next I want you to understand. I was very hungry. Very hungry. I had been underfed and starved for almost 10 months. Food is important to me. I live on it. The lack of food, along with the lack of family, had been my greatest pain in these months. Suddenly, there it was. Food, endless food. Mashed potatoes and gravy. Big piles of meat. Vegetables. Milk. And oh, the baked goodies. Cakes, cookies, muffins. Even pie! You didn't even have to wait just for meal times. There was always a place on that ship where you could find some food. And really, what else was there to do? No letters to read or write. No buddies to swap lies with. Foster only was interested in hearing about farm life in Ferndale for so long, and frankly, Sedro-Woolley was interesting to me mostly for the funny farm it hosted. So Foster and I shared our passion for food. And that is how I gained 60 pounds in three to four weeks. Yes, 60 pounds. Not proud of it of course, but there it is. When I got out of camp I weighed in at about 120 pounds. Maybe I had gained five pounds or so on Red Cross packages. But when I got off the boat, I weighed 182 pounds.

It was certainly not very healthy, but there was another problem with this sudden weight gain that would plague me for many years to come. It seemed to make a liar out of me. At the very time I was putting on all that weight, the world was finding out for the first time about Buchenwald and all the other work and death camps in Hitler's Germany. The famous pictures of striped prisoners with their empty eyes and skin and skeleton bodies were being seen around the world. Buchenwald, as one of the first and largest to be discovered, was making all the headlines, shocking the world with the news about horrible deaths, torture, medical experiments and systematic starvation. So when I quietly told people that I had been in Buchenwald, my suddenly overweight appearance made such a claim hard to believe.

Near the end of our cruise to New York, we came across a reporter on board the ship. He was doing a great service to families of returning POWs by taking their pictures, getting their names and then having them sent by way of his newspaper back to the hometown newspapers of the POWs. That way, the families and the whole town could get news of them, see that they were coming home, and actually see a photo. It was a more efficient system than the Army had for informing POW families. So Foster Perry and I had our pictures taken. And sure enough both the Ferndale Record-Journal and the Sedro-Woolley Courier published the photo of Foster and me. There we were in plain black and white: two fat and happy ex-POWS coming home, including one short, very fat and happy ex-Buchenwald prisoner. I can tell you I did not look like a recent inmate of that dreadful place. And even though my mom knew I wouldn't lie about something like that, I believe to this day she had serious doubts about my claim, at least until I explained to her my over-eating on the ship.

Finally, we arrived in New York harbor, and I watched the Statue of Liberty pass slowly by the ship. It is a beautiful sight and especially meaningful to those who understand what liberty really means and the high price that must be paid for it. It was my mom's birthday, and I so badly wanted to get to a phone finally and tell her I was coming home, that I was fine and to wish her happy birthday. What a sweet present that would make for her! But there were only 15 phones in the room where we could make our calls, and literally 100 guys were waiting in line for each phone. I figured I'd have a better chance in the middle of the night. I woke up at 4 a.m. and sure enough, the lines were down to three or four. I got to the phone and with shaky hands and voice told the operator on the line to ring Mary Moser in Bellingham, Washington. It rang and rang and rang and rang. Come on, mom, I whispered quietly, answer the phone. Certainly she could hear it.

It was one o'clock in the morning on the west coast. She couldn't be gone. Answer, mom, answer!

"Joe? Is that you Joe?" It wasn't mom's voice, it was the operator.

"Yeah, it's me."

"Joe, its Elsie Wood, your neighbor."

"Elsie! I can't wake up mom."

"I know Joe, let me try your Aunt Alice."

"OK, thanks Elsie." I was so relieved and thankful for a familiar, friendly voice, but a the same time I was almost in tears to not be able to talk to mom.

"Hello?" Aunt Alice came on the line, sleepily and frightened.

"Aunt Alice, it's me, Joe." I said.

"Joe! Joe! Is it you?" and she started to cry. I started to cry and could hardly talk.

"Aunt Alice, I tried to wake up mom, but she didn't answer."

"Joe, your mom had a big birthday party, and I think she is pretty tired. I'll see her first thing in the morning Joe and tell her you are coming home! Joe, you are coming home!"

The reality of that hit me right then more than at any other time. I was coming home.

I didn't get a chance to talk to my mom until June 10, when I got off the train outside of Seattle. I boarded the train in New York on June 6 and crossed this great land we call home, for which so many of my generation had paid the ultimate price. I have never looked at my country the same way. I paid a price, sure. But not like so many others. I do think the small price that I paid has made me much more appreciative than perhaps most for the cost of our freedom. It is a great privilege to live in the greatest country, the best country, the world has ever seen.

EPILOGUE

I arrived in Auburn, a little south of Seattle on June 10. I called my mom from the train station and this time she answered the phone.

"Mom, I'm in Auburn," I told her. She was crying.

"I'm coming to pick you up," she said, and in about three hours, there she was, that dear, sweet lady who meant the world to me. She was crying and looked like she had cried all the way from Bellingham to Auburn. Her tough son who had been through hell cried in her arms like a baby.

We didn't make it all the way home without a stop. There was a wedding going on in the tiny town of Bow, about 20 miles south of home. It was a wedding for a distant relative, but a lot of my family would be there. So we just popped in. I was in my Army Air Corp uniform, looking spiffy and quite overweight. There were shocked cries as I walked into the church basement and hugs all around. Then the many cries of, "I heard you were in Buchenwald and POW camp, doesn't look like they starved you after all. Maybe all we are hearing about those camps isn't true." I tried to explain, but how do you explain putting on 60 pounds in a month? I suddenly regretted all those cookies and doughnuts.

I finally made it home to see my sisters and brother. Louise was all grown up and 20 years old. She had been married while I was on leave, before I shipped off to the war. Mom had sold the farm earlier, and my brother Frank had moved in with Uncle Frank Imhof to work on the farm. My brother still operates our old family farm, plus a lot of other land he bought over the years. Little sister Rosalee was then about seven years old and the only one still at home with mom.

After spending a week or two just readjusting to life back home, I started to get a little restless. It wasn't long after I was home that my Uncle John Imhof arranged for me to come and give a presentation to the Ferndale Lions Club about my war experiences. I've never been much for talking in front of a group but I figured what I had been through would be interesting to these folks, and I was eager to share it with them. I told them as best I could about being a fighter pilot, getting shot down and then the horrors of Buchenwald. While I was losing some of that excess weight, I was still on the porky side. I walked out of the meeting after it was done and fell in behind a group of four men who had been in the audience. They didn't know I was right behind them.

"So, what did you think of that?" one asked the others.

"I didn't believe a damn word he said," one of the others said emphatically.

I stopped and felt like someone had stuck a knife in me. That's it, I said. I'm not talking about this stuff again. That decision was confirmed by my encounter with an Air Corps lieutenant assigned to debrief me. I was ordered to Santa Monica, California, because I was still in the Air Corps. My 60-day leave was up, and there was still a war going on in the Pacific. The young officer asked me lots of questions about my experience as a fighter pilot, about getting shot down and what happened to me next. When I mentioned I was sent to Buchenwald, he stopped me.

"No Americans were in Buchenwald," he said flatly.

"Well, I was and I'm an American," I told him equally flatly.

"No, you weren't. There is no record of any Americans being in Buchenwald and if there were we would know about it."

"Well, apparently you don't know about it because I was there, and there was a bunch of other Americans with me."

"I don't know why you are insisting because it didn't happen," he said, closing the conversation.

Why talk about it anymore? To this day, the flags representing the nations of prisoners held in Buchenwald fly over the camp. There are no American flags because there has never been official recognition that a handful of Americans, along with other Allied flyers, were also subjected to Buchenwald's special horrors.

The Army wanted me to continue flying and go to the Japanese theater. But as a POW I had the option of staying home, so I joined the Army Air Corps reserves. That decision almost landed me in the Korean War. As a reserve member they had the right to call me up for active duty within five years. One month after my five years was up, they called me. I was promoted to Captain and the Air Force, now its own branch and separated from the Army, was looking for experienced fighter pilots. They offered to train me in the latest jet fighters — a very tempting offer. I would love to have flown a jet. But I turned them down. My life had taken a different direction. I had become a family man and already had a wife and two daughters.

Girls hadn't played much of a role in my life — other than my mom and sisters. But on the way home from the war, it was inevitable that my thoughts, like those of most of us young men returning home, turned to life after the war. Girls definitely had a place in that picture — or a girl I should say. But who? And how would I find her?

When my mom and I stopped by the wedding in Bow, there was a girl I knew there who seemed very friendly and nice. We danced a little and afterward I asked her out. We went out a few times, and then someone stopped me on the street in town and congratulated me.

"What? What for?" I asked, but somehow I had a sense of what they would say.

"I heard you were getting married. Everyone knows it."

Seems my girlfriend was jumping to conclusions. A couple of dates and she had me tied down already. Or so she thought. This one's going too fast for me, I thought. I called her up and told her we wouldn't be going out anymore.

I needed a little time to adjust to life again, and I was finding the adjustment a little harder than I expected. My mom liked to cook bacon pretty crispy. But the smell of overcooked bacon invoked in me overwhelming fear and dread. It was the crematory in Buchenwald. All my life and to this day, I can't stand that smell. Some memories never fade, and it is surprising how memories can be triggered by certain smells.

It wasn't long after I returned from Santa Monica with the question settled about going to Japan that I started working. I had been a farmer all my young life, but I found a job with the Holland Furnace Company in Bellingham. I was pretty mechanically oriented — as my first flight instructor noted — and fixing furnaces fit me pretty well. It wasn't like the open fields and working with the animals, but I did enjoy the people, and I could also keep to myself when I wanted to.

In November of 1945, a few months after I returned home, my Uncle Frank married the woman that became my Aunt Pat. I was actually close in age to my Uncle Frank, and we were very good friends. I grew up with him and his brothers. At the dance after the wedding I spotted a friend of my sister Louise. Jean Douglas had been at my home several times visiting my sister. I always thought she was kind of cute and was certainly one of the liveliest girls I knew, but it wasn't until the dance that I noticed she had turned into quite a lovely young woman. I was as shy as I could be but, my goodness after all, this was a friend of my sister. What could one dance hurt? I was a lousy dancer, just trying to learn, but Jean seemed willing to help me out and tried to make me look less clumsy than I really was.

We talked a lot about sports because she loved playing softball and baseball and even was a catcher on the Bellingham Bells semi-professional baseball team. They recruited her to play during the war because military duty had called many of the men from the community, and because she was a darn good baseball player. I loved sports too so it made it easy to talk to her. She was friendly, and warm and seemed to like helping me learn to dance. I asked if I could take her home. She said, "Yah!" So I drove her to her home on the Guide Meridian, just south of the Pole Road. On St. Patrick's Day, 1946, we were at a dance at the Seven Cedars in Mount Vernon and I popped the question. Jean and I were married on June 26, almost exactly a year after I returned from the war.

After working at Holland Furnace, I was offered a job at Van's Sheet Metal in Lynden. This furnace company was owned by Chris, Jim and Gerrit Van Andel; Jim was the mayor of Lynden, a small town about 10 miles north of Ferndale. In 1973, the company was bought by two of their bright, entrepreneurial employees, Gary Van Loo and Andy Mellema. The name changed to Andgar Corporation, and I worked for this one company with two different owners for 40 years. I finally retired in 1986, though I helped out once in a while when they needed it for a few years after.

My job was not the reason I declined the opportunity to fly jet fighters. In November 1947, my first daughter, Janet, was born. In 1949, we were blessed with another daughter, Joyce. It seemed a good idea to stick with the letter "J" in the names we chose. Maybe in part because when my mom finally remarried in 1950, she chose to marry a guy by the name of Joe Moser. That was my dad's name — and mine — but no relation. I guess you could say we kind of stick to the knitting in my family. Julie joined us in 1953, our son Joe in 1955 and Jaleen, playing the cleanup spot, arrived in 1959. Now we are blessed to have seven grandchildren and five great-grandchildren.

We went to ball games — endless ball games — by the time our kids and grandkids were playing. We did our work, went to church and lived a grateful, if ordinary, life. We followed the Seattle Mariners and Seahawks, Ferndale High School football and Jean kept her athletic career alive — now with league bowling. I never really shared much of my story with my family. Jean and my children did not know of my time in Buchenwald. They knew that I was a fighter pilot, had been shot down and had been a POW, but that was it. After my painful experiences of not being believed, plus the desire shared by so many of my fellow veterans just to get on with our lives, I kept the story you have read inside. There were times when the memories became painful. Like when the movie "Schindler's List" came out, I really wanted to see it. I made it until I saw the smoke rising from the chimneys of the crematory. I had to leave. In 1982 I went to my first POW meeting in Bellingham. That was when I became reacquainted with Jim Hastin, my buddy through those dark days of the Paris train ride and Buchenwald. He had returned to his hometown of Anacortes, and we renewed a long-lost friendship that was one of the great joys of my life until he died in February, 2005. Talking with Jim and other POW and KLBers (the club of former Buchenwald inmates) like Art Kinnis helped me deal with and start to be comfortable talking about what had happened.

At one of those first POW meetings, I was approached by Bill Lewis, the editor of the Lynden Tribune, to tell my story. I hesitated. Did I want the old wounds to be opened? Did I want more people to say they "didn't believe a damn word I said?" But I said yes and told my story, including my two months in Buchenwald. He wrote the story, and that is how my wife, Jean, found out what the war really was for me. She had to read about it in the newspaper. She jokes once in a while that our marriage has survived a lack of communication.

I'm proud to have served my country, proud to be part of the quickly diminishing group of former POWs. If there is one thing to leave you with, it is that common ordinary people just like you and just like me can once in a while be called upon to show extraordinary courage and strength. And many in those circumstances will have to pay the final price to serve our country and protect our freedom. Please do not forget these people. And never, ever forget the price that many have paid to protect our precious freedom.

RESOURCES

The primary source for the story told here is Joe Moser. He and his wife, Jean, graciously sat through hours of interviews while I probed his memory for those details that would help give life to his remarkable story.

Here are some of the additional books, articles, videos and other material used to help complete the story:

"429th Fighter Squadron: The Retail Gang," by Karl Swindt. 1978. Published by Heritage Publications and South Sacramento Printing
This is the unofficial diary of the 429th Squadon, 474th Fighter Group by their former Intelligence Officer.

"168 Jump Into Hell: A True Story of Betrayed Allied Airmen," by Art Kinnis and Stanley Booker, 1999, published by Art Kinnis
The best resource for the story of the flyers in Buchenwald as it contains an extensive collection of personal accounts of individual survivors, including the stories of their capture in the French Underground. Collected by two survivors. Art Kinnis was also the president of the KLB Club.

"In the Shadows of War: An American Pilot's Odyssey through Occupied France and the Camps of Nazi Germany," by Thomas Childers
A thorough and very well-written story of one of the Buchenwald survivors, Roy Allen, by a well-known WWII historian.

"Shot from the Sky," a History Channel documentary released in 2004.
This mostly accurate documentary includes an interview with Joe Moser and follows the story of B-17 pilot Roy Allen.

"Surviving the German Death March," by Al Hemingway, WWII History Magazine, March 2008, page 60
Tells the story of one survivor of the march from Stalag Luft III to Spremberg.

"Destination Buchenwald," by Colin Burgess
An Australian book detailing the story of the 168 Allied Airmen.

"Fighter Pilot," by Lt. L.C. Beck, published by his parents in 1946
A remarkable personal account, written while hidden by the French Undergound.
It relays the experiences and emotions of an eager young American fighter pilot. Lt.
Beck was one of the two of the 168 who died in Buchenwald. His manuscript was
returned to his parents by those who helped hide him.

"Maybe I'm Dead," by Joe Klaas
A novel based very closely on the death march written by one of the survivors.

"Clipped Wings," by R. W. Kimball, 1948
Stories, poems, cartoons and photos detailing the life of "kriegies" in
Stalag Luft III.

"The Buchenwald Report," translated by David A. Hackett. Westview Press, 1995
Contains first-hand survivor accounts collected by Army intelligence officers days
after the liberation of Buchenwald. One of the most chilling and disturbing records of
inhumanity ever recorded.

"Propwash," the yearbook of class 43-I of fighter pilots in training, Sequoia Field,
Visalia, California.

"Koncentration Lager Buchenwald," article by Jim Gosney, Yakima Herald-Tribune,
August 23, 1991.
An article about Joe and other area survivors relating to the 40X8 rail car on display
in Yakima.

"The Longest Mission," published in 1995 by the Association of Former Prisoners of
Stalag Luft III.
A beautifully presented large-format book of photos and history of the
experiences of POWs in Stalag Luft III.

"P-38 Lightning in Action," by Larry Davis. 1990 Squadron /Signal Publications,
Carrollton, Texas
Photos and illustrations of the P-38 Lightning.

"P-38 Lightning at War," by Joe Christy and Jeff Ethell. Charles Scribner & Sons,
New York.
History and photos of the fighter in action in WWII.

"From Somewhere in England: The Life and Times of the 8th Air Force Bomber, Fighter and Ground Crews in World War II," by D.A. Lande. Motorbooks International Publishers and Wholesales, 1990

"Coming to Terms," by Greg Woehler, Klipsun magazine, Western Washington University, April 2001

Remco Immerzeel, letters and email correspondence, 2007 and 2008
Remco lives in France and has studied the circumstances surrounding the crashes and subsequent stories of many Allied pilots and crew lost in the farmland near Dreux, France. His personal interviews with the French farmers and in some cases, the German soldiers involved, was very helpful in telling this story.